Time-Saving Tips for Teachers

SECOND EDITION

Dedicated to our father, Joe Strohmer, for teaching us by word and example the importance of doing our jobs well but also saving lots of time for family. Also dedicated to Bob, Maria, and Megan Carhart and Jerry Wachter for giving us incentive to work efficiently so we have time to enjoy them.

Time-Saving Tips for Teachers

SECOND EDITION

Joanne C. Wachter   Clare Carhart

CORWIN PRESS, INC.
A Sage Publications Company
Thousand Oaks, California

Earlier versions of Reproducible Forms 57–61 were published in *Classroom Volunteers: Uh-Oh! or Right On!* by Joanne C. Wachter. Copyright © 1999 by Corwin Press, Inc. All rights reserved.

For information:

Corwin Press, Inc.
A Sage Publications Company
2455 Teller Road
Thousand Oaks, California 91320
www.corwinpress.com

Sage Publications Ltd.
6 Bonhill Street
London EC2A 4PU
United Kingdom

Sage Publications India Pvt. Ltd.
B-42, Panchsheel Enclave
Post Box 4109
New Delhi 110 017 India

Printed in the United States of America

Library of Congress Cataloging-in-Publication Data

Wachter, Joanne C.
Time-saving tips for teachers/Joanne C. Wachter, Clare Carhart.-
2nd ed.
    p. cm.
ISBN 0-7619-3914-8 (cloth) — ISBN 0-7619-3915-6 (pbk.)
    1. Teachers-Time management. I. Carhart, Clare. II. Title.
LB2838.8.W35 2003
371.102—dc211

                                                            2003004316

03 04 05 06 10 9 8 7 6 5 4 3 2 1

Acquisitions Editor:	Faye Zucker
Editorial Assistant:	Stacy Wagner
Production Editor:	Melanie Birdsall
Copy Editor:	Kristin Bergstad
Typesetter:	C&M Digitals (P) Ltd.
Proofreader:	Tricia Toney
Cover Designer:	Tracy E. Miller
Production Artist:	Lisa Miller

Contents

About the Authors

Dear Teachers,

I would like to introduce my sister and coauthor, **Joanne C. Wachter.** Joanne started her career in education as an elementary school teacher. She continued her studies, as she worked full-time, to earn her doctorate in education. She then served as language arts supervisor for elementary and middle school teachers in a public school district. This job provided her with much material for this book because she had the opportunity to observe many skilled teachers. She also had to develop organizational skills and time-savers so that she could fulfill her many work requirements and still have time for relaxation and fun.

For the past several years, Joanne has been a full-time textbook writer. She spends her days coming up with creative ideas for teaching language arts in regular education and ESL classrooms. She has had to fine-tune her organizational skills even further to meet challenging deadlines.

As I've watched Joanne in her career, I've witnessed firsthand how one can be very dedicated to and excel at one's job without the job becoming one's total life. I'm sure Joanne's ideas can help you save some valuable time so that you can enjoy your life even more.

Good luck!

—Clare Carhart

Dear Readers,

It is my pleasure to tell you something about my sister, **Clare Carhart.** Clare brings to this book practical ideas from her experience as a high school mathematics teacher. When she first started teaching, Clare was newly married to Bob. The nature of his job was such that he could not bring any work home, so they made an agreement that neither would work at home. This provided my sister with the particular challenge of finding ways to get all her work done by the time she left school. And the answer was not that she could habitually stay late at school, because her school was in an area where it was unsafe to stay after about 5:00 P.M. Therefore, she had to find ways to work very efficiently so she could get all the basics and a few frills done in a short period of time. She did a great job of doing this while also building a reputation as a creative, effective, and caring teacher.

Next, Clare transferred her academic and organizational skills to a community college setting where she taught remedial math. Now, she is working as a coordinator of a church education and youth program . . . while also being a dedicated mom to two little daughters.

I know you will find the ideas she contributed to this book valuable and practical.

Enjoy!

—Joanne C. Wachter

Introduction

Who's Got Time to Figure Out How to Save Time?

Teachers come in many varieties with different talents, interests, and philosophies. Any time a group of teachers gets together, there is lively discussion and professional debate on almost every aspect of teaching. This is true unless you ask, "What is the single biggest problem teachers have?" The answer, then, is a unanimous, resounding, one-word response: "TIME!"

You, as a teacher, need and deserve a secretary and at least one assistant. With that kind of support, you might be able to have a family life, participate in social events, and have time to nurture yourself. However, that kind of support is not likely to be forthcoming in the near future. Instead, relief must come in the form of getting more done in less time and changing some attitudes that get in the way of a healthy, happy life.

This book is packed with practical, tested ideas to help you start to contain your job yet maintain high standards. This book was written for good teachers who want to continue to be good without going crazy. (Teachers who don't care never have a problem with time!)

Browse through the book. Mark ideas that fit your style and needs. Try out a few at a time. Use the ideas as springboards for other strategies or devise variations to meet your particular situation. It is especially helpful to work with a colleague. Above all, take a playful, experimental approach to seeing how you can improve your enjoyment of both your teaching and the other parts of your life.

1

Working Smarter

Most of us were taught to finish our work before we played. But as a teacher, such a work ethic would condemn you to a life without play! You are never going to finish your job. There it is, in black and white. When you picked teaching, you selected a profession that never has a sense of closure.

You cannot say, "Well, I'm finished teaching that child. Now, I'll move on to the next." You never get to sigh at the end of the day, "I'm all caught up. There is nothing else I can think of that needs to be done today, so I guess I'll go home now." Yet these truths are not reasons to grab the Help Wanted ads and see what else you can do with your life. They may, however, impel you to develop some new attitudes.

Try on These Attitudes for Size

Here are three ways of thinking about teaching that may help you set some goals related to "working smarter" so you have more time to do what you want.

1. *You are expected to do a good job, not a perfect job.* You were hired to do one main task: successfully help children learn your subject area of expertise. People will demand that you do well on any aspect of your job that directly relates to this task. They will not demand that you be superhuman and do a perfect job, nor will they insist that you do an exemplary job on the "frill" tasks related to your teaching assignment. You have to admit in your heart of hearts that you know you will not be fired because your bulletin board isn't perfect or because you agreed to be on only two of the three committees on which you were asked to serve.

Acting as if you have to do every aspect of your job perfectly is perfectionism, and perfectionism isn't a virtue. Many people answer the standard interview question about their weak points by saying, "Well, I tend to be a bit of a perfectionist." They think they are answering this negative question in a way that puts them in a positive light, but they aren't. Perfectionism is a bad habit that must be overcome. The perfectionist is not yet skilled at sorting the important from the unimportant and setting priorities. Not all things deserve to be done equally well. Approaching your job with this attitude in mind will help you set logical limits and use your time wisely.

2. *You deserve a fair wage.* Teaching is not a nine-to-five type of job, nor is it a job in which you punch a time clock and get paid by the hour. However, it is still a job. Your employer simply hires you at a fair wage to do an honest job. Your employer does not buy your entire life! The reality is that the smarter you work, the more you get paid per hour. Also, the more efficient you are, the more you're free to enjoy your favorite activities and spend time with your loved ones. Looking at the following case studies will show you how this works. Both of these teachers have been identified as outstanding by their peers and by administrators. The work they do is comparable, and their salaries are $42,000 per year ($1,000 per week for 42 weeks).

Typical week for Mrs. C

Arrives at school 7:45 A.M.
(Teaches from 8:30 A.M. to 3:00 P.M.)
Leaves school—4:00 P.M.
TOTAL SCHOOL HOURS: 8.25

Works at home—none (except for one or
   two emergency situations per year)
Weekends—none
TOTAL HOME HOURS: 0

Equivalent Hourly Wage—$24

Typical week for Mrs. M

Arrives at school 7:30 A.M.
(Teaches from 8:45 to 3:10)
Leaves school—4:30 P.M.
TOTAL SCHOOL HOURS: 9

Works at home—2 hours per night

Weekends—4 hours
TOTAL HOME HOURS: 14 hours

Equivalent Hourly Wage—$17

Based on 16 nonsleeping hours per day for seven days a week, we have 112 available hours per week. Mrs. C spends 41.25 hours working, leaving her 70.75 hours to enjoy the rest of her life. Mrs. M is working 59 hours a week, and giving herself only 53 hours to be with family, friends, and self. The difference between Mrs. C's schedule and Mrs. M's results in Mrs. C getting paid more per hour and having more leisure time. Using some of the techniques in this book would allow Mrs. M to continue to be a good teacher and simultaneously improve her situation.

Again, both these women are doing a superb job of teaching. The only difference is that one is making better use of her time and, therefore, has more time at her disposal.

3. *You deserve a life outside of teaching.* Your family and friends deserve to spend time with you. You were, are, and always will be first and foremost a person. Your role as teacher, while honorable and extremely valuable, is merely a way of contributing to society and earning a living. Take a moment to think about all the other roles you

fulfill: parent, spouse, best friend, church choir member, biking club president. Imagine that your time is limited and you have to prioritize all your roles in order to live a sane, happy life. Well, your time is limited, and you *do* have to prioritize.

You have to slice up the pie and decide who gets what size piece. This may seem like a hard task (and it is), but it is even harder and more frustrating to act as if the pie is limitless when it is not. If you don't deliberately slice up your pie, everyone is going to keep jumping in with his or her fork, grabbing pieces, and making a mess.

Also, if you slice up the pie instead of letting others hack away at it, you can be sure to save good-sized pieces for those who are most deserving. Although your role as teacher is very important, your roles as spouse, parent, and best friend are unique and irreplaceable. Your students will have lots of good teachers, including you, who will put together the pieces of their educational puzzle over the years. On the other hand, you are your children's only mom or dad, and this is their only childhood. You are your spouse's only partner, and this is his or her only life to share with you. You and the important people in your life deserve time together even if you have chosen the honorable profession of teaching.

Changing Attitudes Takes Practice

It is natural to respond to these challenges with a "Yes, but . . ." reaction. Right now, it might seem as if it would be harder to change your mind than put up with the stress of too much work in too few hours. If you find yourself thinking that, you may not be quite ready to make a big attitude change. You may want to start by picking out one little part of something in the previous pages that made sense to you or caused you to think in a new way. Talk it over with a family member or a colleague. Decide on a few small changes you might like to consider and get an ally to support you.

On the other hand, you might feel like you are fed up and want to "get a life," as the popular saying goes. If so, you might be ready to make a major overhaul in your thinking.

2

Communicating Effectively—But Briefly

Much of your time during the day gets eaten up with written or verbal communications that take longer than necessary. Many of these are unplanned. This chapter contains time-saving communication techniques or strategies that in no way detract from being courteous and caring.

• When you receive memos or notes that request an answer, simply jot your response on the bottom of the memo and return it to the sender. Do it immediately, if possible. This hint saves time in that you don't have to go scrounging around for paper, and it reduces waste, too. And last but certainly not least, it gets the paper off your desk so it doesn't accumulate and become clutter.

• Whenever possible, conduct a phone conference or communicate via e-mail rather than a one-on-one. People are more likely to talk a long time if they have gone to the trouble of getting dressed and driving to the school to meet with you in person.

• Have some mindless activity—such as sorting papers or stapling handouts (if you have a quiet stapler)—ready to do while talking on the phone.

• Try to arrange conferences during the day. This may mean a phone conference during a parent's lunch break or before he or she starts work in the morning.

• If you want to discuss specific samples of a student's work in a phone conference, send the parent copies before the call so he or she can review the samples and refer to them while speaking with you.

• If you know that someone with whom you have to communicate tends to be long-winded, correspond by note or e-mail whenever possible to avoid a lengthy in-person or telephone session.

• Make your phone calls a few minutes before your class returns or before a faculty meeting is scheduled to start. This technique allows you to honestly say, "I only have five minutes to talk, but I wanted to talk to you about . . . "

• To avoid "reinventing the wheel," keep a sample of each kind of communication you send out regularly, such as a beginning-of-the-year notice about supplies. When you need to resend the communication, simply make minor changes rather than starting from scratch each time. If possible, do these kinds of communications on a computer so the changes can be made with relative ease. Save all documents you are likely to use again on computer. Also back up on zip drives or CD's.

• If a phone call doesn't require a two-way communication—as when you simply want to confirm a meeting time or tell a parent a child did a good job—call when you are likely to get an answering machine, such as during the day if both parents work outside the home. In this way, your message will be conveyed, and parents will be happy to get the information. This is a win-win scenario no matter how you look at it.

• Photocopy information sheets for the students to fill out (or the parents, if the students are too young) during the first week of school. If or when you need to call a parent or mail something home, you do not have to waste time going to the principal's office. The sheets also provide relevant information about the student, which is readily at your disposal but which you need not memorize (see Reproducible Forms 1 and 2).

• Have a calendar you keep solely for student appointments. These can be meetings that are scheduled at either your request or the student's. If the student keeps the appointment, highlight the name. This provides a quick reference when speaking to a parent or counselor, or filling out progress reports about how often the student comes for help.

• When talking with a parent about a problem, often the parent will become defensive, which shuts down communication or causes the meeting to be long and unproductive. To prevent this situation, use phrases like "I know you agree that we both want what's best for "_____" or "You are the parent and know _____ best, so I want to ask if you think _____ may work better under those conditions."

• Whenever possible, communicate with parents and others in your building through e-mail. Send a note home at the beginning of the year asking parents to provide an electronic address, if they have one and are willing to communicate in this way.

• Make phone calls to parents during work hours—yours and theirs. If the parents cannot be reached when you call, leave a time during school hours when they can return the call. This practice will help keep conversations short and to the point.

• Before the school year begins, create some generic notes for common situations (see Reproducible Forms 3–11). Run off a stack of each and keep them handy for use throughout the year so that you don't have to compose a new note each time.

Of course, you will occasionally want to create a more personalized note, but in other cases, a form will do.

- Another alternative is to use some generic check-off notes when appropriate. Think of the humorous check-off letters you have seen.

> *Dear _____ Mom   _____ Dad,*
> *I am doing _____ fine _____ awful _____ okay.*
> *Your _____ son _____ daughter,*
> _____

Create such notes for positive communications and concerns. This kind of letter lets you send information without taking so much time to write individual messages each time (see Reproducible Forms 9 and 10 for examples).

- Type letters and notes you send out on a computer and save them on a disk. This practice keeps your desk free of paper copies and ensures that you have a copy for future reference.

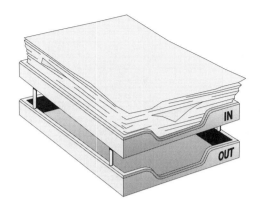

3

Managing Materials

The old adage about "a place for everything and everything in its place" is an important one when it comes to managing instructional supplies. Storing materials and resources conveniently in a predictable place will save you from wasting time looking for items. It will also save you the trouble of running from one end of your classroom to the other to retrieve materials while you are teaching or when you are working on a project during your planning time.

- Store books, guides, and other materials you use for planning near your desk so they are easily accessible without getting up. Store the students' books elsewhere.

- If you don't have bookshelves near your desk, create a book storage area of plastic bins or paper boxes that can be stacked on their sides to form shelves.

- Store materials near where they are used. For instance, have a tin or box of chalk near the chalkboard. Keep markers and transparencies near the overhead projector.

- When you are going to do a project, gather all the materials before you start, just as you would get out all the ingredients for a recipe before you begin cooking. Put the materials in a basket with a handle so you can transport the project easily if you want to work on it somewhere other than your room. Also, having the materials in a basket allows you to easily put them away when your class returns after lunch. You can quickly resume your work later without having to gather materials again.

- Get rid of anything you don't use regularly. Be ruthless! The less you have to take care of or to sort through when you are looking for something, the more time you'll save.

- When you put up a new learning center, take a moment to jot a list of the materials in the center on an index card. Attach the card to the learning center. Assign a student to check the list after the center has been used for the day and notify you if any supplies are needed. If your students are too young to do this, ask an older child to stop by your room at the end of the day and check all of the centers for you. He or she can make a list of materials that need to be replenished for the next day. You may also be able to have him or her secure some or all of these materials from supply closets, offices, or other storage areas.

• Keep a basket of commonly used supplies: stapler, scissors, various pens, frequently needed phone numbers. These will always be ready to quickly transport to a private workspace or to take with you to places when you anticipate that you might have to wait (for instance, at the photocopier).

• Maintain a list of frequently used supplies on your desk and keep a highlighter nearby. Whenever you notice you are low on a particular item, highlight it on the list. This ongoing shopping list will save you from trying to remember what you need or running out of something. Make your own list or use Reproducible Form 12.

• List the names of people who borrow books or other resources from you. This time-saving habit will help you easily relocate the items when you need to use them. Create your own list or use Reproducible Form 13.

• When you put materials away at the end of the school year, do not just dump them in a drawer. This may save time in June but will cost you time in September. Instead, file things neatly and label everything clearly. Your materials will be that much easier to find.

• Use the computer to create bulletin board titles, banners, and the like. You can outline them with markers or mount them on construction paper to add some color. While the document is printing, you can do other work.

• Put your seating chart on an overhead transparency and staple it in a folder. (If you are a secondary teacher, make a folder for each class.) Use the transparency to quickly take attendance by x-ing out empty spots where children are absent. Have a parent volunteer, or a student who finishes work early, transfer the information to your grade book. Erase the marks so you can use the transparency the next day.

• If your teaching area and your work area are in different spots, create a portable desk. A plastic dishpan works great. Always keep chalk, overhead pens, pens, pencils, grade book, and other frequently used materials in it. Load it at the end of each day with all the materials and supplies you will need for the next day. This "desk" will prevent you from forgetting things and wasting time traveling back to your room or work desk during a lesson.

• When you move an item from its usual place (such as taking a file from a cabinet or a book off your shelf), place a note in the space where the material should be returned. Indicate where you have put the material. (For example: "Lent writing workshop file to Pat April 10.") This helps you readily identify where to place the material upon its return. It also prevents undue anxiety when you have forgotten the precise whereabouts of your belongings.

• Masking tape often gives out before the year ends. Try using double-sided or duct tape instead. Another idea is to use staples or modified paper clips (clips you have bent into a hook shape) if you have fabric or corkboard areas. These methods will help you avoid wasting time rehanging materials that fall down.

4

Planning the Week Ahead

Teaching is deceptive. To the unaware observer, it looks as if the main job of a teacher is to spend about six hours a day working with one or more classes of children. But this is like suggesting that an Olympic skater's job is to spend 15 minutes skating. For the skater and teacher alike, the final "performance" is the result of hours and days of hard work. It is important to examine this preparation process carefully to see how time may be used more efficiently.

Planning

On Friday, make a list of things to do the next week, day by day. Try to weigh the days equally. If you work better in the beginning of the week and tend to wear down toward the end, plan more for Monday, Tuesday, and Wednesday. Schedule less on Thursday and Friday. As unexpected tasks come up during the week, add them to your schedule. Tasks that do not have to be done within the week can be added to the bottom of the list. If you finish a day's work and have time, begin another day's work.

Following is an example of a plan for the forthcoming week.

Monday

- Plan week's worth of math
- Plan week's worth of science
- Check students' projects
- Fill out forms for counselor about J. M.

11

Tuesday

- Prepare 3 days' worth of math materials
- Prepare 3 days' worth of science materials
- Record project grades
- Contact book company about sample texts for science

Wednesday

- Prepare 2 days' worth of math materials
- Prepare 2 days' worth of science materials
- Create math test
- Laminate posters

Thursday

- See secretary about field trip
- Assemble materials for science lab
- Photocopy all science and math materials for next week
- Attend C. J.'s IEP meeting at 3:15

Friday

- Assemble and organize math materials for next week
- Assemble and organize science materials for next week
- Grade and record math quizzes
- Call zoo about field trip arrangements

Other Stuff (if time allows)

- Enter quiz averages on grade sheets
- Wash transparencies
- Print banner for bulletin board

In addition, keep in mind the following time-savers. When necessary, adapt these hints to suit your specific needs.

• Have an emergency lesson plan prepared at all times. Use this when you finish a lesson early, when you have to cover for another teacher unexpectedly, or when a lesson has gone haywire. This fallback can be a "mind-bender," a puzzle, a book or poem with discussion questions, or anything else that will work regardless of the students' background.

• Schedule more difficult planning tasks for productive times (for example, a morning planning time if you are a "morning person"). Save less important, more routine tasks for a less productive time when you are likely to feel less energetic.

• Put frequently used statements of objectives and routine directions on charts, sentence strips, or cards that you can hang on the chalkboard or wall so you don't have to rewrite these repeatedly. These materials can be laminated so that you are able to write in page numbers or other customized information. For example,

Students will write to persuade.

Students will read for information.

Read pages _____ to _____ and write a journal entry on _____.

- Discipline yourself to spend all your planning time on the specific tasks you need to accomplish on a given day. Use your breaks in teaching and the time before and after school for these tasks. The rest of your time is yours, to spend as you wish, with the peace of mind that comes from knowing you used your designated planning time well.

5

Assessing Students' Work and Keeping Track of Progress

To know the specific strengths, interests, and areas for instructional focus for even one child is a challenging undertaking. Trying to do this for every area of study for 30-odd elementary children or 130 or so secondary children is a daunting task. This chapter provides some ideas about managing the tracking and recording of youngsters' growth and progress.

• Decide on standards before giving an assignment. Go over these with the students before they begin work, so they will know what you expect. Use the standards to make your grading easier. (See the generic examples for reading and writing standards on Reproducible Forms 14–19.)

• Get students involved in creating the standards with you at the beginning of an assignment. Not only does this practice save you time, but it is an extremely beneficial experience for the kids.

• Let students correct some of their own work. Research has shown that this is a valuable aid to learning, so you need not feel guilty about it.

• Let students respond to or correct each other's papers from time to time.

• Have copies of homework answers, if the assignment has objective answers, to hand out for students to check their own work at the beginning of class. You can circulate during this time and clear up any concerns. Teach students to put the correct number at the top of the page and collect the work. You can then, quickly and at your convenience, see how everyone did and enter grades in your grade book. Save the answer sheets to be used by other classes or for the next year.

- Predetermine the specific things you will correct on particular assignments rather than responding to every element of the paper.

- From time to time, get parents involved in responding to children's homework or other assignments, if possible. Use a form to guide them in making positive comments (see Reproducible Forms 20–22).

- As often as possible, in elementary or middle school, assign homework that involves building responsibility and skills but does not require extensive checking. For instance, students may be assigned to read a certain selection and then discuss one related question with their parents. The parent can simply sign off that the child completed the assignment.

- Stagger due dates for major projects so that all classes are not handing them in at the same time. For instance, if you are an English teacher, you may want to have half your classes doing a writing unit while the other half is doing a literature unit that involves more discussion than written work—and then alternate.

- Keep an observation form with you so you can jot notes about students' progress as you move about the classroom observing individual work and listening in on group work. (See Reproducible Forms 23 and 24 for examples of generic tools you can adapt to your own needs.)

- Use a random sample approach once in a while. That is, randomly select a quarter or a third of your students' papers to correct to get a feel for the general understanding of the class so you know whether you need a lot or a little more practice with a concept. An alternative is to randomly select several items you will correct on each pupil's paper.

- Use the computer to compute grades if it makes life easier. If it slows you down, use another way.

6

Learning to Say No

Probably the most effective, most valuable (and the hardest) thing you can do to save time is learn how to say no without feeling guilty. It is not up to you to do everything, even if no one else volunteers. Furthermore, if you are doing a good job with your most important assignment—teaching—no one is going to fire you for saying no to some extra tasks.

Saying no requires a willingness to maintain a firm stand. For some, it is going to be a significant challenge at first. Maybe you are not even going to believe it is possible to say no in most situations. Trust us: We have both done it successfully and are living much happier lives as a result.

The nature of teaching is such that you will never finish your To Do List. As a dedicated and creative teacher, you will always think of something else you *could* do. But you are doomed to failure and frustration if you maintain a mind-set that demands you actually *do* everything you could.

The challenge is to make that mental shift from managing all the tasks you have to do to managing time. So put yourself on a "work diet." Instead of limiting calories, however, you are going to limit the time spent on working. Decide on a specific time at which you will quit each day. Then, prioritize like crazy.

Plan a week ahead so that wondering what to do tomorrow never causes you stress. Figure out how you will use time efficiently to accomplish what you need to. Focus on the tasks that must get done; forget the frills. If there is time left over, you can do some things from the frills category. But remember, kids in your class do not learn because you create fancy bulletin boards; they learn because you know your subject and because of the caring, compassion, and patience you demonstrate.

This work diet mind-set will change your life, but it will take a major effort on your part. Therefore, you need help. Get a colleague to work on making this shift with you so you can support and encourage one another through the first awkward weeks. Explain what you are doing to family members who would be positive, supportive, and helpful. Get a timer and use it to remind you of your quitting time. Set it for

10 minutes before your deadline, and use these last minutes to figure out an emergency plan for dealing with any necessary tasks that aren't yet completed.

Finally, because this represents a major shift in the way you have probably worked before, set up a reward system for successes along the way. You and your colleague can celebrate at the end of the first week of your work diet by going someplace special or buying yourselves treats.

The following suggestions are designed to help you realistically perform a finite set of responsibilities. They will actually help you to function maximally, to the benefit of all concerned—you, your colleagues, and your students.

• Say no when you mean no. Don't give a reason or try to defend yourself. Simply and cheerfully say, "No, that won't work for me," or "No, I won't be able to do that presentation."

• Do not change your personal plans simply because someone at school or a parent asks you to attend a meeting. Simply say, "I already have a commitment. Is there another time that would work for you?"

• When someone asks something of you, refer him or her to someone else if you know someone who wouldn't mind being asked. For instance, if someone asks you for information about a certain topic, you can say, "Here is one thing that might help you, but you might also want to check my bookshelf or talk to the school librarian." Be helpful with ideas, but let the person making the request do the legwork.

• Do not automatically agree to be on a committee year after year. Think about agreeing to participate on alternate years. You can say, "Thanks for thinking of me. I was on that committee last year. I am going to give someone else the opportunity to do that service this year."

• Be very selective about which committees you join. At the beginning of the year, make an agreement with yourself about the number of committees in which you will participate. Make the number as small as possible and figure out ways to stick to it. Choose committees that are likely to involve working during the meetings rather than having subcommittee "homework" to do between meetings.

• If your boss asks you to be on another committee after you have hit your limit, tell him or her honestly that you are already committed to as many things as you can do without robbing time from the kids in your class. If he or she persists, maybe you can negotiate some kind of limited participation.

• Avoid doing a newsletter. Newsletters seem like a good idea initially, but they are tremendous time eaters. If your administrator mandates that you produce a newsletter, work with your colleagues to do a team, department, or grade publication. Take turns producing it or share responsibility for columns. Ask children in your class or older children who enjoy writing to write some articles. Use as much preexisting material from other newsletters or journals as possible.

• If someone asks you to do something when you are walking down the hall, on the way out the door, or eating lunch, ask him or her to write you a reminder note and put it in your mailbox if you can't answer the request immediately.

- As much as possible, avoid volunteering to do anything unless directly asked. For instance, if you and another person could make a phone call about a field trip, see if the other person offers before you volunteer.

- Buy a pocket calendar with small boxes for each day. This will help you avoid overbooking yourself because there simply won't be space for too many extra engagements per day. Also, when someone else asks you to commit to something and then sees that you are indeed all booked up, he or she is more likely to back off.

- Keep your calendar with you at all times, if possible. In that way, you can set appointments on the spot rather than having to recontact someone later. Also, looking at your calendar during a meeting can help you determine when and if it is realistic to undertake another commitment.

- There is an exception to the previous technique. If you are going to be with someone with whom you do *not* want to make an appointment, don't bring your calendar. Then, if asked for a date to get together, you can make a nebulous statement about thinking that you have something planned for that time, but if he or she calls you, you will check your calendar. Then, when the person calls, you can say you won't be able to make the appointment. It is hard to do that if the person is standing by your side looking at your calendar.

- Block out planning time on your calendar. Write in ink not only your regularly scheduled daily planning time but also other times you intend to use for planning—for example, if you want to use after-school time. Make these notations for planning your regular classes and any additional activities you agree to do, such as presenting a workshop for teachers. Do not be shy about saying, "No, I am already committed during that time," if someone asks you to do something during the time you have marked in ink for planning. Remember, you don't owe anyone explanations or need to defend yourself. Planning time should be a priority on your calendar.

- Whenever you have to bring food for a faculty event, buy instead of make it. If you are particularly concerned about what people will think, become known for bringing a certain dessert from an especially good bakery. You could also do something creative, such as bringing favorite candies from your childhood that will be fun to eat and bring back memories for your peers.

- Say no to yourself when you are demanding perfection of yourself. Most day-to-day tasks do not deserve to be done perfectly. Good enough is good enough in many instances. Try it and see what happens.

- You are not obligated to attend evening or weekend ceremonies or events for your colleagues or students unless you really want to do so. Send a card or buy an inexpensive book as a gift instead. The person will feel acknowledged and will appreciate the gesture, and you will have your evening or Saturday free.

- Do not carry a briefcase to work. If you do, you will be tempted to fill it with work to bring home. Do not take work home with you unless it is an emergency situation. Finish all work for the next week by the time you leave work on Friday. *Never* take work home for the weekend. You need the break in order to be at your best from Monday through Friday.

7

Handling Printed Mail

The next time you collect your mail at school, quickly count how many items are in your mailbox. Multiply that number by the number of days in the school year. For instance, if there are 10 pieces, and your system is in session 180 days, that is 1,800 pieces of mail you must handle. With that kind of volume, it is important that you streamline the process as much as possible.

• Save a few minutes to deal with your mail at the end of each day. This practice helps you handle the job efficiently and avoids a discouraging pileup.

• Deal with your mail as much as possible right at the mailbox area. If you bring it to your workspace, you are likely to get distracted with other tasks and the mail may get "lost" among other paperwork.

• The faculty mailboxes should be situated near a trashcan, recycling bin, table, and, if possible, photocopier. If they are not, talk to the principal or whoever is responsible for these matters to see what it would take to do some rearranging. Once you have that set up, you'll probably be able to handle most of your mail on the spot.

• Keep as little paper as possible. For instance, take your calendar with you to the mailbox and jot down dates from meeting notices into your date book so you can immediately deposit the announcement into the recycling bin.

• Throw out junk mail without opening it. However, if there are certain reputable companies that send out ads or promotions for quality materials—such as our publisher, Corwin Press, which regularly offers books specifically for schoolteachers, or, let's say, a software company that has provided educational programs with which you have been impressed—by all means, skim through the literature. But you do not need to waste time on the endless ads and promotions that are inappropriate for the grades you teach or subjects outside your areas of expertise.

- At the mailbox, sort the mail into piles based on what needs to be done with each piece. In your office or classroom, handle as many of the piles as possible by filing or acting on them so you don't have to touch them again. (See Chapter 15—Creating a Filing System That Saves Time—for ideas about how to store some of these papers.)

- Whenever you deal with mail, try to do one of the following immediately: *handle, file,* or *pass it on to the next person.*

- If you have a meeting as soon as your classes are done, grab your mail out of your box and take it to the meeting. See how much you can sort and handle while you are waiting for the meeting to start.

- Take a pen with you to the mailbox. If you have a memo from the principal asking for some information, jot the answer right on the memo and put it back in his or her box. If something requires your signature, sign it and send it right back to the appropriate party.

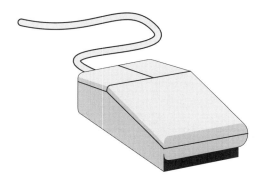

8

Handling E-Mail

If you have access to e-mail at school, it can be a great time saver. If, however, you do not have access at school, do not use e-mail. NEVER, well, almost never, use your home computer to do work related to school e-mail. It will eat up too much of your home time.

- Get e-mail addresses from parents and older students at the beginning of the year.

- Use e-mail only to conduct business, not to "chat" with students.

- Check e-mails once a day. Do not waste time checking in throughout the day.

- If possible, set aside a certain time to deal with e-mail, such as mornings before class or right after school. Set a specific amount of time, perhaps 15 minutes. Anything that cannot be accomplished in that time will need to wait for the next day.

- Try to answer all e-mails as soon as you read them and then delete the original message. This practice will keep your in–box from getting cluttered. Also, when you sign on later, you will know exactly which things you need to address.

- If you do not recognize an address or subject line, delete. Do not waste time on junk mail.

- Do not print an e-mail unless it is something that you need to file away. Most things can be responded to and then deleted. A hard copy is rarely necessary.

- See if your e-mail server has a free date reminder service. If so, you can set up a system to send yourself automatic e-mail reminders of upcoming events such as faculty meetings or special events.

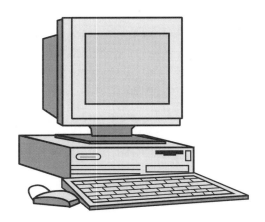

9

Using the Internet to Save Time

The Internet can be a wonderful tool, but it can also be one of the worst time wasters. Make sure you do not fall into the trap of letting the computer gobble up, rather than save, time.

• If you need to research a topic on the Internet, use as specific a title as possible. Do not waste time browsing through loosely related sites.

• Use a good search engine such as GOOGLE (www.google.com) or YAHOO! (www.yahoo.com). Bookmark them so you can access them quickly. Yahooligans (www.yahooligans.com), a search engine for kids, is usually a good resource for finding sites appropriate for students.

• Decide on a specific amount of time that you will use to do a computer search. Set a timer to go off after this amount of time and then sign off when you hear the bell. Having a time limit will motivate you to work efficiently. If you cannot find what you are looking for in the allotted period, perhaps a source other than the Internet would be a better choice.

• Print only as much information from the Internet as you intend to use. Running off extra pages only kills trees needlessly and gives you extra papers to wade through and find a place to store.

• Do not feel pressured to use the Internet for research. If you are comfortable with it, and it helps you save time, use it. Sometimes, however, it is quicker to run down the hall to the media center and find what you need in a book.

• Do work-related Internet research only at work. If you sign on at home for "just a second," you will likely find that your whole evening is gone before you realize it.

• Bookmark sites that you are fairly sure you will use frequently.

• If your community's public library is on the Internet, make use of this resource to do "previsits" to determine whether the books you need are in the collection and whether they are on the shelves. You can even reserve the books you need so that you will be able to swoop in, grab what you need, and be on your way.

• Find one or more online encyclopedias that have the kind and level of information you may be able to use with your class. These can be amazing sources of quick information. There is usually a small annual fee involved, which your school should pay.

• Use online bookstores to find books on specific subjects for certain ages. Take time to read the reviews to be sure that interesting-sounding titles will actually meet your needs. Once you have found titles that look helpful, your school media specialist may be able to help you locate the books in the school collection.

• Do all your computer work at once, if possible. Try to avoid just "getting on for a few minutes" to look up something or to do one task. Keep a running list of things to look up so that when you do sign on, you will use the time in a productive way.

• If your computer has a "sticky note" function on the desktop, use it to keep notes about things you need to do and get. This practice will mean that you have fewer pieces of paper on your desk.

10

Saving Minutes

There are many ways you can save a minute here and there. Just as the pennies add up to dollars if you are careful, so the minutes can add up to hours of free time to spend as you wish—with your family and friends, or in quiet meditation.

• You don't have to use your valuable time doing chores such as taking down bulletin boards. A kid in your class would have great fun doing this. If your students are too young or busy to handle the chore, put a notice outside your door or post an announcement for a child from an upper grade to do it.

• To solve the problem of materials left on the floor at the end of the day, ask a few volunteers to serve as cleanup crew. Tell the kids in the class to be sure to pick up anything they want to keep because the cleaners will be allowed to keep pencils, erasers, stickers, and other items they find during cleanup time.

• When you have permission slips or other materials to collect, label a folder or big envelope. Tape a copy of your class list on the front. Put such folders or envelopes in a bin at the front of the classroom. Teach kids to place their materials in the proper place and check off their names on the list. If your students are too small to handle this, recruit an upper-grade student to stand by and help the little ones turn in their papers and get their names checked off.

• An alternative for keeping track of materials to be turned in is to use a master tracking sheet so that you know at a glance who owes a permission slip, signed papers, or money (see Reproducible Form 25). Highlight names of students as they turn things in so you can see at a glance who is up to date and who needs a reminder.

• Let kids do as much as possible to maintain their room and take care of their own materials. Not only will this save you minutes, it will also foster a sense of responsibility and independence in your students.

• Have a wooden strip put up around the room so that you can tack up students' papers, notices, and posters. This saves the time you'd likely spend rehanging papers when tape doesn't work.

• Don't waste time because of natural forgetfulness. Trust nothing to memory. Write notes to yourself and display them in a place where you won't miss them—in your date book, for instance, or on your door or taped to your key ring.

• Take Polaroid or regular photos of bulletin boards and store them with bulletin board materials so that a volunteer or older student can reproduce a specific bulletin board another year.

• Whenever possible, address problems immediately. Having all the details fresh in your mind will help you handle the job more expediently. In addition, you will not have to sacrifice your efficiency, as you might were you to harbor a worrisome problem in the back of your mind.

• Keep the paperwork for detention or disciplinary action with you at all times stuffed in the back of your grade book. This way you can get it quickly, put the child's name on it, and fill it out later. This cuts down on class time lost while trying to find forms or documenting an incident during class.

• Keep bulletin board materials to use next year. Taking the time to laminate and carefully store the materials will save time in the long run.

• Keep a file folder for each class. Put all homework, passes, notices for students, and other materials unique to the class in the folder. This way you do not have to spend time sorting papers to put things in your grade book.

• To help save time when preparing report cards, make photocopied grade sheets and fill in information when you have time. For example, if the last quiz of the semester has already been given, calculate quiz averages instead of waiting until report card time (see Reproducible Form 26).

• Photocopy generic passes to save time (see Reproducible Form 27). Have the student fill out the pass so you do not have to use up precious class time to do what any individual could do for him- or herself.

• Use students' projects for bulletin boards. For example, the math class that is learning about geometric shapes can draw, color, and label different shapes, which can then be used as a bulletin board. Students who finish their work early can cut letters, take down old bulletin boards, and help to put up new ones. This practice also helps students treat the bulletin boards with care because they have used their time to create them.

• Have students help other students as much as possible. This can cut down on time used for checking homework or assistance given during class time. Remember: You cannot be everywhere at once.

• Test time often seems like a good chance to sit back, relax, and read some articles that have been piling up. Resist this temptation. Instead, make a list of things you want to accomplish, gather all the materials you need, and then work like crazy while the class takes a test. You will be amazed at how much you can get done in one period of uninterrupted time.

- Keep a box of games, puzzles, or "mind-benders" ready for students to use after they finish a test early. This will keep them quietly engaged while the other students finish their work, and you complete the tasks you have planned.

- When you go to the office to make a phone call or photocopy materials, always bring some portable work with you, such as papers to grade or notes to write to parents. If you have to wait in a line or for a machine, you will be able to make good use of your waiting time.

- Ask students to handle as much of your class correspondence as possible. For instance, a student can write a thank-you note to another teacher for sharing materials with the class, or prepare a letter to the media specialist requesting that he or she tape the students reading their own poetry. This practice demonstrates that you trust them, find them capable, and believe they have something to contribute, all of which help build their self-esteem and sense of responsibility—and it saves you time.

- Look at each routine task you have to do and ask yourself how much direct impact the quality of job you do will have on children's learning. If the answer is none, avoid the task or do it just well enough to get by.

- Don't cover bulletin boards with colored paper. The background fades around the papers and pictures you hang on it, and then it needs to be replaced. Instead, leave the cork showing and use a colorful border to make the display attractive. As an alternative, cover bulletin boards with fabric.

- Never spend time cutting out letters for bulletin boards. If you can't get a volunteer to do this for you, write your captions on sentence strips and hang them on the bulletin board. Also, use pictures from commercial kits or cutouts from magazines rather than drawing or tracing your own. These two steps will save lots of time and not have a significant impact on the quality of the students' education.

- If your school district is one that requires community service from students, have students take down or set up bulletin boards, correct papers, photocopy, or do other tasks for community service hours.

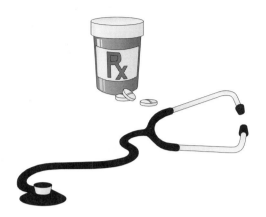

11

Handling
Student Absences

One of the most difficult parts of being a teacher is handling everyone's life at once. When a student is out sick, or in band practice, or on a family vacation, the work often falls to the teacher. You must teach your class, yet also "catch up" the student who has been out. The following are some suggestions that may make this easier and less time-consuming.

• At the elementary level, create a folder for each student where you can store any papers a student missed when absent. When you pass out papers to the class, automatically put a copy in the absentees' folders. At the middle school or high school level, put the papers for an absentee in the appropriate class folder so you have everything on hand when the student returns. Ask a student to jot down notes about any assignments given that day. Store these folders in a bin in a central location in your classroom.

• If you know that someone will be coming into your class late because of, let's say, band practice, seeing the nurse, or some other reason, immediately identify a classmate who sits nearby to get an extra copy of all materials you hand out. Also, ask this student to be prepared to explain what the class is doing when the latecomer arrives.

• Early in the year, send home a letter telling parents your policy about providing schoolwork in advance for planned absences such as family trips. Explain that you will save assignments but can't furnish lessons in advance because lessons are tailored to day-to-day needs. If you wish, tell parents you will furnish some generic review and practice ideas if they wish. (See Reproducible Forms 28 and 29 for examples of generic lessons in reading and writing.) You might want to collaborate with the teachers at your grade level or in your subject area to create several of these that can be shared.

- Maintain a loose-leaf notebook in which homework assignments are recorded. Ask a student to copy each day's assignment with the date. When a student returns from an absence, he or she can go to the notebook and find out the missed assignment.

- When handing out papers, put the name of the absent student(s) on top of blank sheets and then file them in their individual folders or class folders.

- Set a time limit for students to make up missed work, such as a few days or a week. Communicate this policy in the beginning of the year and then stick to it. No one wants or needs a student trying to make up missed work the last week of a marking period.

- Put class work and homework assignments on your class Web page (if you have one) so that students can check from home what they missed.

- Write assignments in your planning book and highlight them. An older student can then use your planning book to find missed assignments for himself or herself.

12

Working With Substitutes

How often have you come to work sick because it was easier than making substitute plans? There will be times, no matter what, when you will need to be absent. Here are some ideas that might make it an easier experience.

- If you know that you will be out for a planned appointment or inservice, try to arrange for your class to join another class for a group activity. This approach allows learning to continue. It also results in the substitute being paired with a teacher who is familiar with the school procedures and students. At some other time, you can reciprocate by letting the other teacher's class join yours when he or she needs to be out.

- If you are feeling ill at the end of the day, leave the next day's work (as much as possible) in your "plans for substitutes" file on your desk.

- Inform students and the substitute that all work will count as a grade. Perhaps, even leave something that will count as a quiz or test grade. This practice will help students take the assignment seriously.

- Whenever you finish a unit of study, have students create questions (and answers) to be made into a quiz to be left in a sub file. This material will serve as a review, and students will be interested because they helped create the materials.

- Leave work that students can correct themselves. If this is not possible, use a multiple-choice assignment so it will be easy to grade when you return. Use Scan-Tron sheets, if you have this capability.

- Make five days' worth of plans to be kept in a file cabinet that can be accessed by a substitute teacher. Use work sheets or activities that provide review. With an unfamiliar teacher, students tend to benefit more from a review lesson than from the introduction of new material. This approach will also decrease discipline problems.

- When you create lessons for a substitute teacher, be sure to give directions for all work to be self- or peer-corrected during class time that day. This provides immediate feedback for students—and you won't come back to a batch of old papers to grade.

- Use a fill-in-the-blank planning frame to create lessons for substitute teachers. (See Reproducible Form 30 for guidelines. See Reproducible Forms 31–50 for examples.)

- Get together with the other teachers in your department or at your grade level. Request that each person create a special-interest or review lesson appropriate to what you teach. Bring snacks and make it a fun occasion. Duplicate all the lessons generated so that all participants have a copy of the complete set to use for substitute plans.

13

Working
With Volunteers

What if you went to the hospital and found out that one of the sweet little ladies or gentlemen from the hospital volunteer group was going to remove your appendix? Imagine the surgeon telling you that because the hospital was afraid its volunteers would be bored with the routine tasks, such as transporting patients in wheelchairs and delivering meals, doctors decided to do those things while volunteers performed surgery.

This situation is laughable, yet it is the kind of thinking often used in dealing with school volunteers. Teachers end up having to do clerical tasks while untrained folks are permitted to work with children.

There are many activities that volunteers can do that are interesting and worthwhile and that free you, the professional, to spend more time doing what you were trained to do. Make use of these suggestions, and adapt any to suit your particular needs.

• Use Reproducible Form 51 to find out what types of activities interest volunteers.

• On Back to School night, or whenever you meet parents for the first time, have them fill out a parent volunteer form (see Reproducible Form 51) and leave it with you that night. It may be your only chance to get volunteers. Also, that sheet will give you information about whom to contact for what so you don't waste time.

• Instead of planning new activities each week, teach volunteers (or see if your reading specialist will instruct them) to do a few important generic tasks that will need to be done all year. For instance, teach them how to

- Read to a child or small group
- Listen to a child read

   – Discuss a story the child has read
   – Talk about a factual article the child has read
   – Confer with a child about his or her writing
   – Practice math facts with a child

• Keep directions for each task in a notebook (see Reproducible Forms 52–55 for some sample directions for volunteers). Each time the parent who specializes in a given task comes into your classroom, you can simply provide a list of students to see individually and direct him or her to the appropriate notebook page.

• Use a standard scheduling sheet to attach to work to be done by volunteers (see Reproducible Form 56 for a sample of such a sheet). Keep these materials in a standard location so volunteers will be able to check for the task that you need them to do without interrupting the lesson in progress.

• Instead of planning for and contacting volunteers yourself throughout the year, recruit one enthusiastic, capable parent to serve as volunteer coordinator for your classroom. Have this person work with your whole group of volunteers to carry out routine jobs you need done. Each person can have a specialty such as bulletin boards or planning for special projects.

• At the beginning of the year, identify a group of several volunteers to be "travel agents" for the class. Each time you want to plan a field trip, meet with your travel agents to discuss your ideas and what tasks need to be done to prepare. These volunteers can contact the site, find out about costs, recruit chaperons, make nametags for the students, find out about transportation, and handle other details. A coordinator from the group can communicate with you about updates and decisions that need to be made.

• Ask a parent to be your library-materials specialist. Whenever you are ready to start a new unit or project, give him or her a list of books, topics, or authors and the range of reading levels of your group or class. Have the parent work with the school and public librarian to collect the materials you need.

• If you teach a primary grade, post a Help Wanted notice in the hallway out-side your classroom. On it, advertise for older students to help you with particular jobs. For example:

Two fifth graders needed to staple packets after school today.

• Provide some training for the various roles you wish volunteers to play in your classroom. Investing a small amount of time in the fall will make it possible for your volunteer program to run efficiently all year. See Reproducible Forms 57 through 61 for training ideas. These forms are reproduced from *Classroom Volunteers: Uh-oh! or Right On!*, another Corwin Press book by Joanne Wachter. The book provides many other tips for working with volunteers.

• Get a group of parents to create and maintain a publishing center. They can be responsible for all aspects of typing and binding students' writing. As an alternative, get one parent to agree to coordinate this effort using older children or volunteers at a local senior citizens' center or similar facility. (See Reproducible Form 62 for a simple method of binding books.)

- Ask a volunteer to be responsible for gathering and shopping for supplies for special projects or events.

- At the beginning of the year, ask an artistic parent to coordinate a Bulletin Board Artists group. This can be a small group of volunteer adults or older children who would take your sketch of an idea and perform all tasks related to taking down the old bulletin board display and turning your sketch into a reality (see Reproducible Form 63 for an example of a planning sheet to give to the Bulletin Board Artists).

- Ask parents to update the class Web page, if you have one. Listing assignments, highlighting upcoming events, and uploading pictures (with parental permission) are all things a volunteer can do to save time for you.

AGENDA

• Test Scores
• New Texts
• Homework Policy

14

Making the Most of Meetings

Do you sometimes feel you are in the business of attending meetings instead of the business of teaching? For educators, the meetings seem endless: faculty meetings, parent meetings, special education meetings, team meetings. For the most part, you have no control over how many meetings you must attend, but you can take control of some aspects of meetings so that they can be more beneficial and less aggravating to you.

• Carry forms that need to be filled out, grades that need to be entered, or other "mindless" work with you to meetings. Meetings usually start late, so you can get work done while you wait rather than wasting time.

• To avoid getting stuck in an "endless" meeting, tell the person in charge of the meeting that you will have to leave at a specified time. Knowing that there is a limit to the time available usually helps the person conducting the meeting to use the time efficiently or to address those agenda items that pertain to you early in the discussion. Although you may not be able to set limits such as this with your administrator, this practice is effective when meeting with parents, other teachers, or specialists.

• If someone asks to meet with you during your planning time, suggest the last half of the time. For instance, if you have planning time from 1:00 until 1:40, say you can meet at 1:20. This approach assures that you will have some time to do your work and that the meeting cannot run on because you will have to go back to your class.

• When someone asks to meet with you, go to his or her office or classroom. This allows you to have more control over when you leave, whereas if someone comes to your room, you have to wait until he or she is ready to leave to conclude the meeting.

• When you cannot avoid meeting in your own room, you can signal the end of the meeting by standing. Another technique is to glance at your watch. When the other person notices and asks if you have to leave or have another commitment, you can express your regrets and say you do.

• If someone asks you to meet, you can say, "Okay, but I only have _____ (specify a number) minutes. Let's use that time and then see if we need more at a later date." People almost always manage to confine their business with you to the time you suggest and seldom need to continue the meeting at a later time.

• When you attend a meeting, throw all extraneous papers or pages of handouts you won't need into the trash as you leave. If there is no trash can, leave the papers that you do not need to keep on the table. The person who handed out the materials may be able to use them for another audience. Discarding handouts before you leave a meeting saves you from having to figure out what to do with them hours, days, and weeks later.

• Sort the rest of the handouts into "read" and "action" piles while you are there. Use Post-it notes to mark the parts of handouts you need to read or act upon later.

• When you attend a conference, take index cards or notepads and a file folder to store information you want to keep. Be very discriminating, however. Do not save anything unless you are *sure* you will use it later.

• Take your calendar to meetings. Put dates on your calendar so you won't have to try to remember or deal with extraneous handouts or reminder notes.

• Work with your team to make team meetings efficient. Suggest at least handwritten agendas or lists of specific questions or issues to discuss so meetings will be productive.

• Whenever possible, do tasks assigned at the meeting then and there. For instance, fill out a survey that you have just been handed.

15

Creating a Filing System That Saves Time

Knowing where everything is saves not only time but frustration and embarrassment. Having all your papers that are worth saving at your fingertips provides a feeling of control. The filing system explained in this chapter also helps you meet deadlines.

Try this three-part filing system. You will never lose an important paper nor will you waste time trying to find something you need.

Reference Files

Make a notebook or file of frequently needed information such as phone numbers and schedules. Be sure these resources are within reach as you work at your desk.

Storage Files

Maintain a file cabinet in which you store information not needed on a weekly basis. Store folders containing handouts for units, school policies, tests, and other things you must keep for yearly use.

This cabinet does not have to be within reach of your work area. Take time at the end of each year to clean it out and ruthlessly discard anything that you will not need the following year.

If you are unsure about throwing something out, toss it in a box. Write the date on the lid and put the box in a closet. Throw out the box if you haven't touched it in a year.

Working Files

Create the following file folder system:

- One folder for each month of the year
- A series of folders numbered with the days of the month, 1 through 31

Keep these folders in a drawer or bin at the desk or table where you work. Whenever you get a piece of paper that you cannot act on immediately, file it in the appropriate folder. Each day, check the folder for the day to see what you have to handle before the day is done. Just before the first day of each month, check the folder marked with the name of the upcoming month. See what can be done immediately. Sort out the rest to go into day-of-the-month files.

Following is a scenario to show how the daily system works:

At the end of the day on Monday, November 7, the following materials are some of the items you find on your desk. Here is how you can use the filing system to handle them.

Materials

- Papers to hand back for self-checking tomorrow
- Notice about a faculty meeting in December
- Master of a handout you used today and want to save to use when you teach again next year
- Note from a parent about calling

File in (respectively)

- Working File 8 (for November 8)
- Working File marked December
- Storage file marked with the name of the unit or handout
- Working File 11 (for November 11)

Other Filing Tips

- Use a different color file folder for each subject or course you teach so that you will know immediately what each folder contains. For instance, if you are an elementary teacher, all language arts ideas can go into blue folders, all math into red, all science into green, and so on.

- Organize your curriculum files by units of study or, if you follow a book closely, by book chapters so that everything for the teaching of a particular unit will be together.

- If you have files that correlate with a specific text, and you will no longer be using that text, get rid of the materials. You may think you will use them in the future, but rarely do they exactly fit with the new materials.

- Keep a beginning-of-the-year file for student information sheets, notices about materials students will need to provide, procedures for classroom rules, and other paperwork you always use in the first few days of school.

- Keep midterm and final tests only one semester. This is long enough to settle any disputes. When you file the most recent exams, throw out the previous ones to save space and time.

- Keep a folder marked Wish List. Drop into it information about any materials you would like to have but cannot purchase at the time. When your principal comes around with end-of-year funds to be spent, you will be ready with your list.

- At the end of the year, go through all files and destroy anything that you will not use next year. No one wants to do this in June but if you do not, it will never get done and files will become cluttered, which will slow you down later.

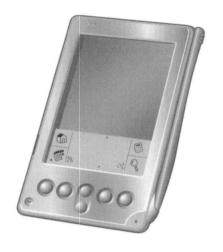

16

Using Personal Digital Assistants (PDAs)

Personal Digital Assistants (PDAs) are wireless handheld computers that some people swear by and others have absolutely no interest in. If you do not have one, there is no need to feel that you need to rush out and get one. If, however, you have a PDA and are competent in using it, it may save a few minutes here and there.

• If you are going to use a PDA for scheduling, make sure you carry it with you always.

• Use your PDA to take notes at meetings.

• If you are not skilled at using a PDA, do not use one. Trying to figure out the machine during the school year will only waste your time. Learning to use this technology and figuring out how it can be applied to your job may be a better project for the summer.

• Program your PDA with all parents' phone numbers as well as the phone numbers of places you go annually on trips.

• If you are using a PDA for scheduling after-school tutoring sessions, note not only with whom you will meet and when but also what you will be working on. This will allow you to notice when more than one student needs tutoring on the same topic so you can schedule them together.

• If you like using a computer for your lesson plans, download the plans from your computer to your PDA. Take the PDA to class with you rather than a plan book.

• If you are using a PDA for all your data, it is highly recommended that you download the information regularly. This practice will protect you from losing all your records if your PDA gets lost, stolen, or broken.

17

Avoiding and Managing Distractions

If you ever counted up all the time lost when you are interrupted by someone who says, "Do you have a minute?" you would be astounded. Not only does it take time to deal with the distraction, but precious moments and momentum are also lost in regaining your concentration. There are many techniques for tactfully avoiding and minimizing the valuable time lost to distractions.

• Discipline yourself to think of planning time and after-school time as serious work time rather than time to socialize. The more you get done in school, the more time you will have to socialize at home with your family and friends.

• Find a secret place to work during planning times and after school. An unused conference room, secluded corner of the media center, or classroom on the outskirts of the building reduces the chances of being interrupted by drop-in parents and other teachers.

• Move your desk so that it is not visible from the door. Work with no light if you have sufficient windows or use a small desk lamp and turn out the overhead lights so people will think you are not in and, therefore, will not disturb your concentration.

• Gently teach people that you don't want to be interrupted when you are in the middle of a project. If someone comes to your classroom and asks you for something, kindly say "I am in the middle of some thing right now. Would you jot me a note so I remember to get what you need as soon as I can?"

• If someone drops by and says, "Do you have a minute?" say, "I only have about three minutes and then I have to . . ." This will help the person be conscious of containing his or her message so that you can get back to what you were trying to do.

• When someone in the office calls over the public address system to say you have a phone message during planning time, don't necessarily feel you have to go running, especially if the phone is not near your classroom. Ask the office to get the number and reason for calling. (Sometimes, when the person states the reason for calling, it will become clear that someone else needs to answer the question anyway.) Once you pick up your phone message and see what the person wanted, save time by responding with a quick note or leave an answer on his or her answering machine, whenever possible.

• If someone interrupts you and asks you to do something, it is okay to say, "I can't right now. How about Wednesday before class?" If you stop every time someone asks you for something, you train people to believe it is okay to interrupt you at any time.

• If you are interrupted while you are writing something, say, "I just want to finish this so I don't lose my train of thought." If you are grading papers, put your finger on the place where you were working on the paper and say, "I don't want to lose my place." Messages like these will help people be mindful that they need to avoid keeping you too long. If they say they didn't realize you were busy and offer to leave, smile warmly and thank them, and then go back to your work.

• If you have someone coming in to see you and you suspect they will take up an unreasonable amount of time, ask a colleague to stop by at a specified time and say something like, "How much longer do you think your meeting will be? I need to see you as soon as you are done."

• When you are working on a project and must stop to do something else or cannot continue until someone else takes an action, jot down a few words on a Post-it note and attach it to your work to remind yourself where you were. This practice will help you resume work quickly when you return to it rather than waste time trying to figure out where you left off. Examples:

> *Waiting for principal's okay*
>
> *Add worksheet to packet*

• If you get caught by someone who wants to complain, shorten the conversation by not adding any complaints of your own. Simply listen until the person runs down, which will take less time if you are not adding fuel to the fire.

18

Coping With the Parts of the Job You *Hate!*

There is no getting around it: Work is hard. That's why it is called work and not play! As long as you accept a paycheck, you are going to have to do some things you don't enjoy, but there are ways you can deal with the toughest parts so that they don't interfere with your positive attitude about the job.

- Do tasks you don't like as soon as possible so you don't waste energy dreading them.

- Swap parts of the job you hate with a colleague. For instance, maybe one of your peers would agree to make a bulletin board for you if you made some phone calls about a field trip for him or her. Perhaps your administrator would set aside a few minutes during a faculty meeting for everyone to list his or her three least favorite teaching-related tasks to see if any deals can be worked out.

- If you can't avoid some jobs you hate, give yourself a reward for completing them.

- If the task you detest is long and complicated, break it up into smaller parts. Give yourself a little break after each part. As an alternative, make a deal with yourself that you will work on it only so many minutes at a time until it is completed.

19

Keeping Up With Professional Reading

Do you feel guilty every time you look at the ever-growing pile of journals and professional books that accumulate in your home and classroom? The ideas in this chapter will help you think about professional reading in ways that may make it more manageable and less guilt producing.

• Team up with a few colleagues. Each of you can subscribe to a different journal related to what you teach. Each person will be responsible for reading only one magazine each month and sharing the best three ideas with the others.

• Instead of trying to tackle the entire journal, as soon as the publication arrives, pull out or photocopy several articles you want to read and put them in a reading folder. Donate the journal to a library or offer it to a colleague. You will have gotten some benefit from it, but it won't be sitting around whispering, "Read me, read me," to your guilty self. If at some later point you need that edition, you can always track it down through the library, the media center, a colleague, or its publisher.

• Who said you have to read every professional book you buy? You can buy them simply for the purpose of having them on your shelf for reference without pressuring yourself to read each one as soon as you get it. When you need the information in it, you will have the book available and can use it at that point.

• When a journal comes in, very quickly skim the few articles that sound most interesting. If they look like they could be helpful, ask a parent volunteer to tape record the articles so that you can listen to them while you commute. This process could turn into a schoolwide effort in which a small group of parent volunteers produces a listening library for all the educators in your building. Not only will this offer teachers another option for keeping up with professional reading, but the parents who tape the materials will be learning more about current concepts in education so they can be advocates for changes you are making.

- Decide that waiting time at school will always be professional reading time. Take your reading folder or a journal with you whenever you might have to wait five or more minutes.

- Have professional journals delivered to your school, not your home. Otherwise, they will be "invading" your home and tempting you to spend your leisure time reading professional materials.

- If you use public transportation to get to and from work, use this time to read educational journals.

20

Treating Yourself
as a Professional

Professional: engaged in or worthy of the high standards of a profession. Designated or of a school . . . offering instruction in a profession. Earning one's living from an activity . . . not normally thought of as an occupation. A person who does something with great skill.

—Webster's New World Dictionary

You deserve to have the image of yourself as a professional planted firmly in your mind. You worked hard to get the training that entitles you to be called a professional. You spend your days making challenging professional decisions that affect the present and future well-being of children and their families. Keeping this well-earned vision of yourself in mind will help you stand firm about the conditions necessary for you to maintain your positive attitude about your job so that you can do the best for the kids in your care.

- Dress in a professional manner. It may seem silly, but if you dress as a professional, you will have an advantage. Parents, other teachers, and students will view and treat you differently than if you wear jeans and a T-shirt. Dressing for work also helps some people to feel empowered to say no when they must, or to voice their concerns and needs.

- Preserve your lunchtime. How many business people do you know who would skip lunch to work? Work like crazy before school, after school, and during all planning times but take off during lunchtime. Eat a good lunch, talk with friends about topics other than school and students, and relax. This routine will give you something to look forward to during the morning, and you will be rested and ready to face your afternoon work.

- Remember at all times that you are a professional. Many believe that those who cannot do, teach. However, if you truly believe you decided to teach because you have knowledge and a talent for helping kids to learn, students and parents will view you differently and respect you, your time, and your opinions more.

- If possible, team up with a colleague who teaches the same subject or grade. People in business rarely work alone because they know that two heads are better than one. Meet in the beginning of the week with this teacher to plan the next week's studies and list all materials needed. Next, divide up the work. Agree that all work will be done by Friday afternoon so that all is ready and waiting for the forthcoming week. Working together not only cuts down on the workload but also encourages creativity.

- Commit yourself to going to one high-quality conference per year and set a goal of bringing back three ideas. If you set such standards as this, you will continue to learn and grow as a professional without overwhelming yourself by thinking you have to collect and implement every good idea at the conference.

- Join a professional organization such as the National Council of Teachers of Mathematics or the International Reading Association. These are sources of readily available ideas, training, and connections with people who can share insights, stories, and hints for avoiding burnout.

- If you present a workshop, turn the information into an article to submit for publication, or vice versa. This practice lets you get double benefit for your effort.

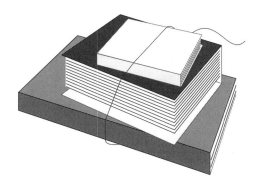

21

Resumes/Portfolios

Although you may not be looking for a different teaching job now, you may eventually find that you need or want to move on. For example, your school may lose positions or you may want to apply for another position within your own school. In either case, you will need a resume. It is much easier to keep an up-to-date resume rather than try to find time to create one when you are facing an application deadline. Every professional should keep a copy of his or her resume on a computer and update it regularly. Putting together a portfolio also gives you a professional edge when trying to get a new job or transfer.

- Save a copy of your resume and portfolio on disk or CD.

- Every time you publish an article, present at a conference, take a class, or complete a degree, make sure you add the accomplishment to your resume before it has time to slip your mind.

- If you have a lesson that goes really well, do not forget to add a description, lesson plan, or picture of it to your portfolio.

- Add photos to your portfolio of activities you did with your class. Make sure you delete dated material as you add new items. Remember when using photos, you must have parental permission for any students that show clearly.

22

Creating a Pleasant Work Atmosphere

Every task is a little easier when done in a pleasant environment. Gather a few items that give you comfort and make them a part of your workspace. This suggestion will make the time you spend working on planning, grading, and other activities more enjoyable. A pleasant area will also remind you of the good things ahead if you get your work done efficiently and have more time to relax by yourself or with family and friends.

Try adding some of the following items to the area where you work to make it more inviting and to make the time you spend there pleasant and productive.

- A CD or tape player so you can listen to your favorite relaxing or invigorating music while you plan lessons or respond to students' assignments

- A supply of your favorite healthful snack

- A nice pen you enjoy using, such as one of the disposable fountain pens available at stationery stores

- Flowers or plants

- Restful posters or pictures on the wall you face as you sit at your workspace

- A favorite mug for a soothing cup of tea or juice while you work

- A dish of potpourri that you enjoy

- A pillow or cushion for your chair

- Pictures of your family or friends (to inspire you to finish your work fast and get home)

- An attractive, inexpensive lamp with soft light, so you can turn off harsh overhead lights

- Spaces or containers to put away all your work and materials so you do not feel overwhelmed when you return to your workspace the next time

23

Discussing Schoolwide Commitments

This book has focused on various ways that you can take control of your own time. If you try even a few of the ideas in the previous chapters, you will feel a notable improvement in the time it takes to do your job. If you want to feel an even greater impact, get other professionals in your school interested in how to better manage time. If the administrator is willing to work with you on this, you may be able to change some practices over which you now have little influence. Maybe the faculty at your school would get excited about a yearlong focus on ways to use time efficiently. When everyone is conscious of this goal—supporting one another, working together to create and share the tools and systems that enable everyone to function to the max—there is no telling what could happen!

• Ask your administrator to consider committing to no interruptions during class unless an emergency happens. Announcements can be made at the beginning of the day and at the end. Any phone calls can be taken by a secretary and messages left in teachers' mailboxes. Students can be given passes during homeroom if they must miss class to see the counselor, nurse, or other person during class time. Perhaps the principal would be willing to try this approach as an experiment for a week or two and then discuss its pros and cons.

• Find out if it would be possible to have a page typed by the school secretary to announce deadlines, meetings, field trips, and other important items instead of having intercom announcements. Each teacher can pick up (or better yet, read and leave) a copy when entering the building each day.

• Talk to the principal and colleagues about the idea that homeroom and daily after-school experiences such as waiting for buses are not playtime. Students could be required to do homework or read silently. Those who do not want to do these activities can act as student aides. They can take down bulletin boards, copy materials, check learning centers for missing parts, and so forth. This routine would help teachers get some work done and free them from baby-sitting. This idea may be met with some initial resistance from certain students, but with time would be accepted.

• Talk with administrators about letting teachers suggest inservice training that would be of the most use to them. To avoid the duplication of effort that is all too common among educators, at least some of the professional development time could be devoted to group problem solving and teamwork on creating instructional units and materials; there is no sound reason that teachers must invent all solutions and plans individually.

• See if the principal would be willing to have schoolwide meetings once a month rather than weekly. This decision would mean a longer meeting, but in the end it saves time. When meetings occur less frequently, people think more carefully about what needs to be addressed and what could be done in another way.

• As a faculty, discuss with your administrators barriers to efficient job performance. For instance, in some schools, teachers are not allowed to use the photocopying machines or other equipment. Keep the conversation positive but push to remove these obstacles; present teachers as responsible, professional adults.

24

Closing Thoughts

We hope you have found some useful suggestions in this book. And we hope that we have conveyed the importance of taking on a new way of thinking about setting priorities and limits while still doing a good job. Working with your colleagues to support one another as you find some ways to work more efficiently will make this process even more rewarding and more enjoyable. Also, you will have support when you run into a tough problem or temporarily slip back to some old attitudes.

The whole premise of this book is that you deserve not only to teach in a way that makes you feel proud but also to have a life outside of your job. Remember to use the time you save *not* to do more work but to relax and enjoy the peace and happiness of time spent doing things you enjoy with the people you love.

Resources

Reproducible Forms

STUDENT INFORMATION SHEET—ELEMENTARY AND MIDDLE SCHOOL

Name _____

Nickname _____

Address _____

_____

Home phone _____

E-mail address _____

Home Contact

Parents (legal guardian) _____

Parents' work phones _____

Best time to contact parents _____

Interests

Hobbies _____

Teams _____

Favorite subjects _____

Birthday _____

STUDENT INFORMATION SHEET—HIGH SCHOOL

Name _____

Nickname _____

Address _____

_____

Home phone _____

Parents' e-mail address _____

Student's e-mail address _____

Home Contact

Parents (legal guardian) _____

Parents' work phones _____

_____

Best time to contact parents _____

Interests

Hobbies _____

Teams _____

Favorite subjects _____

Plans after high school _____

SUPPLIES LETTER TO STUDENTS' FAMILIES

Date _____

Dear Family,

Your child will need the following supplies for a project we are doing: _____

_____

_____

_____

_____

_____

_____

We will need these materials by _____. If you have any questions or will

be unable to get these supplies, please let me know as soon as possible. Thank you for your help

and support.

Sincerely,

ACHIEVEMENT LETTER

Date _____

Dear _____,

I want you to know that your child, _____, did a wonderful job

today on _____. This achievement

represents a lot of hard work, which I know makes you proud. Thanks for your continued

support.

Sincerely,

IMPROVEMENT LETTER

Date _____

Dear _____,

Your child, _____, has shown great improvement in

_____. I appreciate this hard work and know you will,

too. Thanks for your support.

Sincerely,

EFFORT LETTER

Date _____

Dear _____,

Your child, _____, has been working very hard at being productive and

responsible in class. That kind of effort deserves special recognition and appreciation!

Sincerely,

PHONE CONFERENCE LETTER

Date _____

Dear _____ ,

I would like to set up a phone conference or a meeting with you to discuss _____

_____

Some good times for me to talk with you uninterrupted would be from

_____ until _____ on _____

_____ until _____ on _____

or

_____ until _____ on _____

Please call the school office and leave a message about which time is most convenient for you. I look forward to hearing from you.

Sincerely,

EVENT INVITATION LETTER

Date _____

Dear _____,

I would like to invite you to attend a special event in our classroom. The event is _____

_____.

It will take place from

_____ until _____ on _____.

We hope you will be able to join us.

Sincerely,

STATUS NOTE TO PARENTS—GOOD PERFORMANCE

Date: _____

Dear _____,

This letter is to inform you that your son/daughter

　　　_____ has been doing a great job.
　　　_____ works well with others.
　　　_____ did very well on his/her test/quiz.
　　　_____ is showing much improvement.
　　　_____ is cooperative in class.

I have expressed my appreciation to your son/daughter and know you will also want to congratulate him/her for a job well done. If you would like more details about this accomplishment, please call the school and leave a message. I will return your call. You can also respond with a note or e-mail message if that would be better for you.

Sincerely,

Additional comments:

STATUS NOTE TO PARENTS—POOR PERFORMANCE

Date _____

Dear _____,

This letter is to inform you that your son/daughter

_____ is not cooperating in class.
_____ needs to improve his/her behavior.
_____ needs to improve his/her work skills and grades.
_____ did not do as well as expected on his/her last test/quiz.
_____ is not currently working well with others.

I have spoken with your son/daughter about this situation and ways we can all work together. If you want to speak with me further about this matter, please call the school and leave a message. I will return your call. You can also respond with a note or e-mail message if that would be better for you.

Sincerely,

Additional comments:

FIELD TRIP PERMISSION FORM

On _____, your child's class will be going to

_____. We will leave at _____ and return at approx-

imately _____. All money and permission slips will be due by _____.

(If cost is a problem, please contact me.)

I give my son/daughter, _____, permission to participate in the field

trip described above.

_____

Signature   Date

SHOPPING LIST

Get From School Storage	Buy at a Store		Get From School Storage	Buy at a Store	
_____	_____	Staples	_____	_____	Paper clips
_____	_____	Pencils			Rubber bands
			_____	_____	
_____	_____	Lined paper	_____	_____	Art paper
_____	_____	Crayons	_____	_____	Paints
_____	_____	Chalk			Stick-on notes
			_____	_____	
_____	_____	Copy masters	_____	_____	Thumbtacks
_____	_____	Folders	_____	_____	Index cards
_____	_____	Legal pads	_____	_____	Notepads
_____	_____	Markers	_____	_____	Pens
_____	_____	Overhead transparencies			

Other supplies:

Item	Location
_____	_____
_____	_____
_____	_____
_____	_____
_____	_____

LENDING LIST

Material	*Borrower*	*Date*
_____	_____	_____
_____	_____	_____
_____	_____	_____
_____	_____	_____
_____	_____	_____
_____	_____	_____
_____	_____	_____
_____	_____	_____
_____	_____	_____
_____	_____	_____
_____	_____	_____
_____	_____	_____
_____	_____	_____
_____	_____	_____
_____	_____	_____
_____	_____	_____
_____	_____	_____
_____	_____	_____
_____	_____	_____
_____	_____	_____
_____	_____	_____
_____	_____	_____
_____	_____	_____
_____	_____	_____
_____	_____	_____
_____	_____	_____

STANDARDS FOR NARRATIVE WRITING*

It is effective to share these standards with students before they write.

A story that deserves A TOP GRADE must have these qualities:

_____ Interesting beginning that grabs attention

_____ Clear setting described with vivid images

_____ A central problem or goal that is the focus of the action with all the story events relating to it

_____ Characters that are revealed through what they say, do, or think

_____ Dialogue that sounds real and moves the story along

_____ Adequate elaboration so the reader is not confused or left wondering about major details

_____ A memorable ending

_____ Interesting style and word choice

_____ Spelling, capitalization, punctuation, and language usage that are very good for the child's grade level

A story that deserves AN AVERAGE GRADE must have these qualities:

_____ Somewhat interesting beginning

_____ A clearly identified setting that is described with some vivid words

_____ Characters who are described by the writer and may reveal themselves somewhat through what they say, do, or think

_____ A clear problem or goal with most of the story events relating to it

_____ Fairly realistic dialogue that moves the story along in most cases

_____ Enough elaboration so that most details the reader needs are furnished

_____ An ending that is somewhat interesting

_____ Reasonable style and word choice for the age of the child writing the piece

_____ Spelling, punctuation, capitalization, and usage that look as if the writer made some attempts at editing and corrected most of the mistakes you would expect for a child at this grade level

A story that would deserve A LOW GRADE without further revision and proofreading has the following qualities:

_____ An uninteresting beginning

_____ An unclear setting or a setting that is stated but not described

_____ Characters who do not yet come alive through their actions, thoughts, or words

_____ An unclear central problem or goal with a confusing succession of events

_____ Unrealistic dialogue that does not advance the story

_____ Insufficient details to satisfy the reader

_____ An uninteresting or abrupt ending

_____ Lack of style or interesting word choice

_____ First-draft spelling, capitalization, punctuation, and usage that do not look as if the writer attempted to proofread

* These standards have been used successfully with upper elementary through secondary schoolchildren. Obviously, the standards should be applied with more leniency when grading elementary papers.

STANDARDS FOR POETRY*

It is effective to share these standards with students before they write.

A poem that deserves A TOP GRADE must have these qualities:

_____ Clearly focuses on an event, person, place, object, or feeling

_____ Has a rhythm that is obvious when the poem is read aloud

_____ Uses literary devices (figurative language, alliteration, personification, etc.) in interesting ways

_____ Evokes sensory images

_____ Evokes a feeling or mood

_____ Uses punctuation, capitalization, and spacing that enhance the final effect and make the message clear; uses spelling that is very good for the child's grade level

A poem that deserves AN AVERAGE GRADE must have these qualities:

_____ Has an identifiable focus on an event, person, place, object, or feeling

_____ Most parts have a rhythm that is obvious when the poem is read aloud

_____ Uses literary devices (figurative language, alliteration, personification, etc.) with at least some success

_____ Evokes sensory images in at least one or two parts of the poem

_____ Parts of the poem evoke a feeling or mood

_____ Uses punctuation, capitalization, and spacing in ways that do not seriously interfere with the message; uses spelling that meets expectations for the grade level

A poem that would deserve A LOW GRADE without further revision and proofreading has the following qualities:

_____ Has no clear focus on an event, person, place, object, or feeling

_____ Does not have the rhythm of poetry when read aloud or focuses heavily on rhyming words but does not describe anything or tell a story

_____ Does not use literary devices or uses them in a way that causes confusion

_____ Does not evoke sensory images

_____ Does not evoke a feeling or mood

_____ Uses punctuation, capitalization, spelling, and spacing in ways that confuse the reader

* These standards have been used successfully with upper elementary through secondary schoolchildren. Obviously, the standards should be applied with more leniency when grading elementary papers.

STANDARDS FOR EXPLANATORY WRITING*

It is effective to share these standards with students before they write.

An explanatory piece that deserves A TOP GRADE must have these qualities:

_____ Interesting beginning that grabs attention

_____ Topic that is clear from the beginning with all sentences clearly relating to it

_____ Organization that makes the piece easy to read

_____ Adequate elaboration so the reader is not confused or left wondering about major details

_____ A memorable ending

_____ Interesting style and word choice

_____ Spelling, capitalization, punctuation, and language usage that are very good for the child's grade level

An explanatory piece that deserves AN AVERAGE GRADE must have these qualities:

_____ Somewhat interesting beginning

_____ Topic that is clear with most sentences clearly relating to it

_____ Organization that does not confuse the reader

_____ Enough elaboration so that most details the reader needs are furnished

_____ An ending that is somewhat interesting

_____ Reasonable style and word choice for the age of the child writing the piece

_____ Spelling, punctuation, capitalization, and usage that look as if the writer made some attempts at editing and corrected most of the mistakes you would expect for a child at this grade level

An explanatory piece that would deserve A LOW GRADE without further revision and proofreading has the following qualities:

_____ An uninteresting beginning

_____ Unclear topic with a mixture of details

_____ No clear organizational pattern

_____ Insufficient details to satisfy the reader

_____ An uninteresting or abrupt ending

_____ Lack of style or interesting word choice

_____ First draft spelling, capitalization, punctuation, and usage that do not look as if the writer attempted to proofread

* These standards have been used successfully with upper elementary through secondary school children. Obviously, the standards should be applied with more leniency when grading elementary papers.

STANDARDS FOR PERSUASIVE WRITING*

It is effective to share these standards with students before they write.

A persuasive piece that deserves A TOP GRADE must have these qualities:

_____ Interesting beginning that grabs attention
_____ A point of view that is clear from the beginning with all sentences clearly relating to it
_____ Points that are so sensible that they would be hard to argue against
_____ Organization that makes the piece easy to read
_____ Adequate elaboration so the reader is not confused or left wondering about major details
_____ A memorable ending
_____ Interesting style and word choice
_____ Spelling, capitalization, punctuation, and language usage that are very good for the child's grade level

A persuasive piece that deserves AN AVERAGE GRADE must have these qualities:

_____ Somewhat interesting beginning
_____ A point of view that is clear with all sentences clearly relating to it
_____ Many points that are so sensible that they would be hard to argue against
_____ Organization that does not confuse the reader
_____ Enough elaboration so that most details the reader needs are furnished
_____ An ending that is somewhat interesting
_____ Reasonable style and word choice for the age of the child writing the piece
_____ Spelling, punctuation, capitalization, and usage that look as if the writer made some attempts at editing and corrected most of the mistakes you would expect for a child at this grade level

A persuasive piece that would deserve a LOW GRADE without further revision and proofreading has the following qualities:

_____ An uninteresting beginning
_____ Unclear point of view, with the writer seeming unsure of which position he or she is taking
_____ Points that are not very convincing
_____ No clear organizational pattern
_____ Insufficient details to satisfy the reader
_____ An uninteresting or abrupt ending
_____ Lack of style or interesting word choice
_____ First-draft spelling, capitalization, punctuation, and usage that do not look as if the writer attempted to proofread

* These standards have been used successfully with upper elementary through secondary schoolchildren. Obviously, the standards should be applied with more leniency when grading elementary papers.

STANDARDS FOR ASSIGNMENTS RELATED TO READING OF STORIES

These standards can be used to assess and grade journal entries or other written responses to open-ended questions about a story that has been read. These standards can also be applied when you listen to the comments made in literature discussion groups. It is effective to share the standards with students before they read the material.

A response that deserves A TOP GRADE

_____ Shows the child understood complex aspects such as theme, mood, symbolism, and the author's message
_____ Connects elements of the story to the child's own life and experiences
_____ Comments on the author's style and effectiveness in relation to the development of the story

A response that deserves AN AVERAGE GRADE

_____ Shows the child understood the basic idea of the story and enough of the details to make sense of the plot
_____ Connects the elements of the story to the child's life in at least a surface manner
_____ Gives a reaction to his or her feelings about the story

A response that would deserve A LOW GRADE without further rereading and revision

_____ Shows a misunderstanding of the basic point of the story and/or confuses basic important details of the story
_____ Does not yet connect the story to his or her own life
_____ Does not yet react to the effectiveness of the story or feelings it inspires

These standards are appropriate for use with upper elementary and secondary schoolchildren.

STANDARDS FOR ASSIGNMENTS
RELATED TO READING OF SOCIAL STUDIES,
SCIENCE, OR OTHER CONTENT AREA TEXTS

These standards can be used to assess and grade journal entries or other written responses to open-ended questions about a selection that has been read. These standards can also be applied when you listen to the comments made in discussion groups. It is effective to share the standards with students before they read the material.

A response that deserves A TOP GRADE

_____ Shows the child has a sophisticated understanding of the concepts discussed in the reading

_____ Connects elements of the selection to the child's own experiences and other concepts that have been addressed in previous classes

_____ Brings up authentic questions the child has after the reading or comments on areas for further study and investigation

A response that deserves AN AVERAGE GRADE

_____ Shows the child understood the basic idea of the concepts presented in the selection

_____ Comments on how at least one concept from the selection relates to previous learning

_____ Shows the child is able to identify some part of the selection was confusing to him or her

A response that would deserve A LOW GRADE without further rereading and revision

_____ Shows a misunderstanding of the most important concepts in the selection

_____ Does not yet connect the information in the selection to his or her previous learning

_____ Shows the child is unaware that he or she is not comprehending the main concepts of the selection

These standards are appropriate for use with upper elementary and secondary schoolchildren.

PARENT HOMEWORK RESPONSE SHEET—ELEMENTARY AND MIDDLE SCHOOL GRADES

1. Provide a time and place for your child to do homework.

2. When the assignment is complete, have the child spend 5 minutes proofreading for and correcting spelling, punctuation, and other mechanical errors.

3. Go over the homework with your child and jot down some ideas on this sheet.

    − What are 3 things done well on this assignment?

    − What are 3 things that need practice?

Thanks for your input.

Parent's signature _____

Date _____

PARENT RESPONSE TO HOMEWORK

Date _____

Child's name _____

How long did it take your child to do this homework?

What is one thing you noticed that he or she did very well?

What is one thing you noticed that I need to help him or her practice more?

What is one thing that pleased you about your child's work habits while doing this assignment?

What is one work habit for him or her to focus on next time?

What else would you like to tell me?

Thanks for your input.

Parent's name _____

HOMEWORK ASSIGNMENT—PARENT INPUT SHEET

	Fantastic	*Progressing*	*Still Needs Help*	*Comments*
Understanding of the skill being practiced				
Work habits				
Use of time				
Ability to explain what he or she was doing				

Child's Name _____

Parent's Signature _____

Date _____

Thanks for your input.

OBSERVATION OF SKILLS IN GROUP WORK

Date _____

Objective _____

_____

Names of Children in Group	Skills	Observed Yes/No	Comments

IN-DEPTH OBSERVATION OF ONE CHILD

Name _____ Date _____

Skills

Can do independently	Can do with help	Can't do yet

Interactions With Others

Particular strengths	Areas of coaching for further growth

Other Notes

FORM FOR TRACKING PERMISSION SLIPS AND MONEY DUE

Item Due												
Due Date												
Names												

GRADE SHEET

Student _____ Quarter _____

Average	*Percentage of grade (in decimal form)*	*Points awarded*
Tests _____	× _____	= _____
Quizzes _____	× _____	= _____
Homework _____	× _____	= _____
Projects _____	× _____	= _____

Total   _____

Letter Grade   _____

Behavior Grade   _____

STUDENT PASS

This pass is to allow _____ to come to Room #

_____ at _____.

Date _____

Time student left _____

Teacher's initials _____

STUDENT PASS

This pass is to allow _____ to come to Room #

_____ at _____.

Date _____

Time student left _____

Teacher's initials _____

STUDENT PASS

This pass is to allow _____ to come to Room #

_____ at _____.

Date _____

Time student left _____

Teacher's initials _____

CONTENT AREA READING PRACTICE FOR CHILDREN WHO ARE OUT OF SCHOOL BECAUSE OF A FAMILY TRIP

_____ Please have your child do the marked items.

_____ Please choose _____ items below for your child to complete.

_____ Find a magazine article that in some ways relates to the trip you are taking. Have your child read it and write down three things he or she learned from the article and comment on how these related to the trip.

_____ Have your child read a newspaper article related to local news of the area you are visiting. Ask him or her to write a few sentences telling how the information in it compares and contrasts to something that might happen in your community.

_____ Ask your child to read a brochure from your trip. (If the reading level is too challenging, you may read it to your child.) Have your child create his or her own brochure for the same site. Challenge your child to make the brochure appeal to children.

_____ Have your child check out a nonfiction library book that in some way relates to your trip. Ask him or her to make a chart to keep track of how much he or she reads each day. From time to time, have your child tell you something interesting he or she has read in the book.

_____ (Other idea)

Thank you.

WRITING ASSIGNMENT FOR CHILDREN WHO ARE OUT OF SCHOOL BECAUSE OF A FAMILY TRIP

These activities not only provide good practice in the writing skills we are learning in class but also give your child a chance to have fun writing and learn something from your trip.

_____ Please have your child do the items marked below.

_____ Please choose _____ items below for your child to complete.

_____ Ask your child to write a story that is set in the location where you are visiting.

_____ Have your child write a letter to a family member or friend telling about one event that happened on the trip.

_____ Challenge your child to write about something he or she learned about or learned to do on the trip.

_____ Have your child create comic strip pictures and text to show what happened each day of the trip.

_____ Ask your child to keep a trip journal, spending a few minutes each day writing down the best memory of the day.

_____ (Other)

Thank you.

USE OF SUBSTITUTE PLANNING FRAMES

Planning frames are meant to streamline the job of preparing plans for substitute teachers when you must be away from your classroom.

- The plans can be used over and over by simply changing the reading matter or writing assignments given.

- Variations are built into each plan so you can meet the individual needs of your students and provide variety when you reuse the frames.

- Most of the creation of the plan is already done. Simply make a photocopy of the blank form, fill in the required information, and leave the frame for your substitute.

- These plans provide worthwhile, high-quality "generic" lessons that are beneficial to students at any time of the year. They can be put in place for the time you are out and then you can resume what you are doing when you return.

- The lessons can be made shorter or longer depending on how long you expect to be away from your classroom.

- The lessons are built to provide you with information about how the children performed (Substitute Teacher Response Form) without the need for you to grade papers when you return. All work is discussed in class so children get feedback during the class period.

Other thoughts:

- Create a few plans and keep them on file for emergency use.

- Use the models furnished in this book to adapt or generate planning frames for your own subject and grade level if these are not a perfect match with your needs. Create the frames with colleagues in your department or on your team so no one has too much to do.

SUBSTITUTE PLANNING
FRAME—READING A SHORT STORY

Objective: Children will read a story and expand their comprehension of the story by predicting, responding to high-level-thought questions, and developing vocabulary.

Materials

_____ Book _____

_____ Story on page _____ of the following book _____

_____ Prediction Sheet *(Before copying the sheet, fill in the number of a page near the middle and near the end that would make reasonable stopping points for predictions)*

_____ Thinking Sheet *(If you wish to assign certain items, check these on the master before copying)*

_____ Word Map

_____ Substitute Teacher Response Form

Before Reading

1. Hand out the Prediction Sheet to each child.
2. Direct students to look at the cover or, if the story is in an anthology, the first page.
3. Give them time to fill out the first prediction. (If you are working with primary-grade children, this step can be done orally, or you can record their ideas on chart paper.)
4. Have several volunteers share the first prediction.

During Reading

1. Explain to the children that they will be stopping at 2 other points to make predictions. Point out the page numbers. (If working with primary-grade children, you read with them to the middle prediction point and then, as a group, discuss their predictions before reading on the end.)
2. Tell children they will also have a Thinking Sheet to jot down any thoughts while they are reading.
3. Hand out the Thinking Sheet and point out the kinds of notes they can jot down. Make 1 of the following assignments.

    _____ Jot down notes about all the items that have been checked on the sheet.

    _____ Make comments about items that especially interest you.

(For primary-grade children, do not hand out this sheet. Instead, use it as a reference for yourself in generating discussion during and after the reading.)

    _____ Provide quiet reading time. *(For primary children, you may need to read chorally.)*

After Reading

1. Discuss the Prediction Sheets.
2. Use the Thinking Sheets to do the following:

Primary grades

_____ Conduct a discussion of the story between you and the children

_____ Have students create a picture based on a discussion of the best part or the part that reminded them of something in their lives

Intermediate Grades

_____ Conduct a discussion of the story between you and the children

_____ Provide the basis for small group discussion among the children (if they are used to this kind of independence)

_____ Provide the basis of a journal entry about the story

3. Have children fill out the Word Map

_____ In class and discuss it

_____ In class and be ready to discuss it tomorrow

_____ For homework and be ready to discuss it tomorrow

Primary-grade children can be asked to copy an interesting word they can read from the story and illustrate it. These can be shared and discussed.

Closure

Ask children to indicate on a scale of 1 to 5, with 5 being the highest, what they thought of the value of the story. Ask a few to defend their answers.

PREDICTION SHEET

Looking at the title and the front cover, I think this story will be about	Which of your predictions came true? Which did not?
because	
After reading to page _____, I predict	
because	
Near the end of page _____, I predict	
because	

THINKING SHEET

_____ The part of the story I liked the best was

because

_____ The story reminded me of (another story or my experience)

because

_____ I would like to hear my classmate's opinion about

_____ It was confusing when

_____ The part the author wrote the best was

because it

Other ideas about the story:

WORD MAP

Pick a word from the story that you think is interesting or that your classmates would think is interesting. Put it in the box in the middle of this sheet. Fill out all the other boxes.

What do you think about when you hear this word?

What are some words that mean almost the same thing?

How does the author use the word in a sentence?

How would you use the word in a sentence?

SUBSTITUTE TEACHER RESPONSE
FORM—READING A SHORT STORY

Group/Class _____

How well did the children do on each activity?	Great	Okay	Needs work
Prediction Comments:			
Thinking Sheets Comments:			
Follow-Up to Thinking Sheets Comments:			
Vocabulary Comments:			

Other notes:

Thank you.

SUBSTITUTE PLANNING FRAME—READING
SCIENCE, SOCIAL STUDIES TEXTS, OR
OTHER NONFICTION MATERIALS

Objective: Children will review background knowledge, read a selection to increase their knowledge, and expand their comprehension of the selection.

Materials

_____ Selection on page _____ of the following book_____

_____

_____

_____ Know and Learn Sheet
_____ Vocabulary Sheet *(Fill in vocabulary before making copies of the handout)*
_____ Using What You Know Sheet *(Fill in topic before making copies of the handout)*
_____ Substitute Teacher Response Form

Motivation and Prior Knowledge

1. Introduce the topic by

_____ Asking a question
_____ Showing a picture
_____ Showing an object related to the topic
_____ Other

2. Hand out the Know and Learn Sheet. Ask children to think about the topic and list 2 things they believe they know about it.
3. Ask for volunteers to share some responses. Do not comment on the accuracy of their ideas at this point.

(For primary children, have a discussion and record their ideas on a chart or overhead transparency.)

Setting a Purpose

1. Direct students' attention to the part of the sheet that asks for their questions about the topic. Give them a few moments to jot down questions.
2. Tell them they will be reading a selection about the topic for the purpose of checking out what they have said they know and seeing if they can get their questions answered.
3. Hand out the Vocabulary Sheet.
4. Ask students to fill out the middle column by telling what they think they already know about each word. It is okay if they have to guess. Do not allow use of dictionaries at this point.

(This work may be done orally or on a group overhead transparency or chart by primary grade children.)

Introducing the New Information

Introduce the new information by

_____ Having children read independently

_____ Reading it to them

_____ Having them read with partners (if they are used to this kind of experience)

Follow-Up to the New Information

1. Allow a few moments for children to give you their general reaction to what they have read and ask about any confusing parts.

2. Direct their attention back to the Know and Learn Sheet. Give them directions for completing the sheet.

_____ Give directions for each part and have them complete it before going on.

_____ Give directions for all parts and allow them a longer block of time in which to work.

Directions

- Check off the ideas that were confirmed. *(Review the meaning of* confirmed.*)*
- Write in the corrected or expanded idea they got from reading or listening for ideas that were not confirmed.
- Have them decide whether any of their questions about the topic were addressed and jot down the answers in the appropriate spaces.

(Primary-grade children will do this as a group while you record their ideas on the overhead transparency or chart.)

3.   Have children comment on how well the selection addressed the topic.

4.   Clear up any misunderstandings that remain from what they originally thought they knew about the topic.

Vocabulary Development

1. Ask students to look again at the Vocabulary Sheet. Have them add to or correct their understandings of the words. Encourage them to look back at what they have read. Do this activity

_____ Independently

_____ In pairs (if they are used to working cooperatively)

_____ As a class activity (if working with a primary grade)

2. Conclude discussion of the vocabulary by sharing some results and clearing up any misunderstandings.

Closure/Homework

Assign children to complete the Using What You Know Sheet.

_____ During the last 10 minutes of class or

_____ For homework

In either case, have students prepare to share their responses the next day. (Primary-grade children can draw pictures or act out how they will use the information.)

KNOW AND LEARN SHEET

The topic for study is _____

What do I think I already know about this topic?	The author confirmed my idea.	The author gave me a new idea about that.

What are some questions I have about the topic?	The author did not answer my questions.	The author answered my question by saying:

Some other things I learned about the topic are:

VOCABULARY SHEET

Word	I think this means	After reading, some other ideas I have about the meaning are:

USING WHAT YOU KNOW SHEET

How can you use what you learned in class today in your other classes?

What are 2 other things you would like to learn about this topic?	How could you find out?
1.	
2.	

How can you use what you learned in class today outside of school?

SUBSTITUTE TEACHER RESPONSE
FORM—READING A NONFICTION SELECTION

Group/Class _____

How well did the children do on each activity?	Great	Okay	Needs work
Know and Learn Sheet Comments:			
Vocabulary Sheet Comments:			
Using What You Know Sheet Comments:			
Other notes:			

SUBSTITUTE PLANNING
FRAME—WRITING A STORY

Objective: Children will create a story using the stages of planning, drafting, revising, editing, and sharing.

Materials

_____ Story Planner
_____ Filled-out example of the Story Planner on an overhead transparency
_____ Peer Response Sheet (Fiction)
_____ Editing Sheet (Fiction)
_____ Substitute Teacher Response Form
_____ Chart paper and marker (for primary grades)

Planning

1. Discuss the topic of the writing with the children.
_____ A story about an experience they have had _____

_____

_____ A story related to a selection they have just read _____

_____

2. Introduce the Story Planner. Show the filled-out example and explain what each part means.
3. Give children time to plan their stories.
_____ Whole group discussion for primary grades
_____ Individual work for intermediate grades

(If this plan is to be used over more than a day's time, give children time to respond to each other's plans in pairs.)

Drafting

1. Encourage children to use their Story Planners to write their first drafts.
2. Allow time for drafting.
_____ Intermediate/secondary students will work independently.
_____ Primary children will work together to dictate a story you will record on the chart paper.

Revising

Hand out the Peer Response Sheet (Fiction) and direct students to complete it.
_____ If the lesson is to extend over several days, have students meet in small groups or pairs to read each other's stories and fill out the form with ideas.

_____ If the lesson is to be completed in 1 period, have each child simply check over the sheet to see if it provides ideas for any changes he or she wishes to make.

_____ If working with a primary class over several days, pick 1 or 2 items for the students to consider regarding whether they could make changes to make their writing even better.

_____ If working with a primary class for 1 day, skip this step.

Editing

Handle editing in the following way.

_____ For intermediate/secondary children working with you over a period of days, hand out the editing sheet and have them help each other to do a careful check.

_____ For intermediate/secondary children working with you for 1 day only, hand out the editing sheet and tell them you will give them 5 minutes to make as many changes as they can. (You might want to offer some kind of small reward as an incentive.)

_____ For primary children, mention editing points as they dictate. (For example, We are getting ready to start a new sentence. What kind of letter do we need to use? Who can tell us how to spell _____? How should we end this sentence?)

Closure and Homework

Ask a couple of children to share what they have written. For homework, assign intermediate/secondary children to

_____ Make a final copy

_____ Share their stories with someone at home

_____ Prepare to share their stories with the class tomorrow

STORY PLANNER

Place where the story will happen _____

Time when the story will happen _____

How you will get the reader interested at the beginning _____

_____

The main character will be _____

Some qualities the character will have _____

Quality   How will the reader know the character has these qualities?

_____   _____

                                       _____

_____   _____

                                       _____

What the character will try to do in the story _____

_____

_____

Steps/events the character will go through to do this:

The way the story will end _____

_____

_____

_____

_____

_____

PEER RESPONSE SHEET (FICTION)

1. What do you like about how this story is written?

2. What are some questions you still have after reading this story?

3. How interested did the beginning of the story make you? Why?

4. How interesting was the ending? Why?

EDITING SHEET (FICTION)

Check for each of the following:

_____ Sentences begin with capital letters.

_____ Sentences have correct ending punctuation.

_____ Sentences express complete thoughts.

_____ Names start with capital letters.

_____ Quotations are punctuated properly.

_____ Paragraphs are indented.

_____ Words are spelled correctly.

SUBSTITUTE TEACHER RESPONSE
FORM—WRITING A STORY

Group/Class _____

Parts of the Writing the Children Did With Ease	**Comments:**

_____ Using the Story Planner

_____ Writing first drafts

_____ Revising their ideas

_____ Editing their writing

_____ Sharing their writing

Skills For Further Practice	**Comments:**

_____ Using the Story Planner

_____ Writing first drafts

_____ Revising their ideas

_____ Editing their writing

_____ Sharing their writing

Thank you.

SUBSTITUTE PLANNING FRAME—WRITING
A SCIENCE, SOCIAL STUDIES, OR OTHER
CONTENT-RELATED PIECE

Objective: Children will create nonfiction writing using the stages of planning, drafting, revising, editing, and sharing.

Materials

_____ Nonfiction Planner
_____ Overhead transparency of the Nonfiction Planner
_____ Peer Response Sheet (Nonfiction)
_____ Editing Sheet (Nonfiction)
_____ Substitute Teacher Response Form
_____ Chart paper and marker (for primary grades)

Planning

1. Discuss with the students the topic of the writing related to science, social studies, or other curriculum areas.

_____

2. Introduce the Nonfiction Planner. Talk through and demonstrate putting in the topic and some subtopics. Jot a few notes about   each subtopic. Show how you would decide on the order in which to address the subtopics.
3. Give children time to fill out the Nonfiction Planner for the topic of their writing.
_____ Whole group discussion for primary grades
_____ Individual work for intermediate grades

(If this plan is to be used over more than a day's time, give children time to respond to each other's plans in pairs.)

Drafting

1. Assign children to use their Nonfiction Planners to write the first drafts of their writing.
2. Allow time for drafting.
_____ Intermediate/secondary students will work independently.
_____ Primary children will work together to dictate ideas you will record on the chart paper.

_____

Revising

1. Hand out the *Peer Response Sheet (Nonfiction)* and direct students to complete it.

_____ If the lesson is to extend over several days, have students meet in small groups or pairs to read each other's stories and fill out the form with ideas.

_____ If the lesson is to be completed in 1 period, have each child simply check over the sheet to see if it provides ideas for any changes he or she wishes to make.

_____ If working with a primary class over several days, pick 1 or 2 items for the students to consider regarding whether they could make changes to make their writing even better.

_____ If working with a primary class for 1 day, skip this step.

Editing

Handle editing in the following way.

_____ For intermediate/secondary children working with you over a period of days, hand out the editing sheet and have them help each other do a careful check.

_____ For intermediate/secondary children working with you for 1 day only, hand out the editing sheet and tell them you will give them 5 minutes to make as many changes as they can. (You might want to offer some kind of small reward as an incentive.)

_____ For primary children, mention editing points as they dictate. (For example, We are getting ready to start a new sentence. What kind of letter do we need to use? Who can tell us how to spell _____? How should we end this sentence?)

Closure and Homework

Ask a couple of children to share what they have written. For homework, assign intermediate/ secondary children to

_____ Make a final copy

_____ Share their writing with someone at home

_____ Prepare to share their writing with the class tomorrow

NONFICTION PLANNER

Fill out the topic and each box. Then, go back and decide the order for your ideas. Circle 1st, 2nd, 3rd, or 4th to show when you will write about each.

Topic: _____

I will write about this 1st, 2nd, 3rd, 4th	*I will write about this 1st, 2nd, 3rd, 4th*
One subtopic I will write about is A few things I will include are	Another subtopic I will write about is A few things I will include are

Topic: _____

I will write about this 1st, 2nd, 3rd, 4th	*I will write about this 1st, 2nd, 3rd, 4th*
I will also discuss the subtopic A few things I will include are	I will also discuss the subtopic A few things I will include are

PEER RESPONSE SHEET (NONFICTION)

1. What information did you learn from reading this writing?

2. What are some questions you still have after reading this writing?

3. How interested did the beginning of the writing make you? Why?

4. How interesting was the ending? Why?

EDITING SHEET (NONFICTION)

Check for each of the following:

_____ Sentences begin with capital letters.

_____ Sentences have correct ending punctuation.

_____ Sentences express complete thoughts.

_____ Names start with capital letters.

_____ Headings are capitalized correctly.

_____ Captions are correctly capitalized and punctuated.

_____ Quotations are punctuated properly.

_____ Paragraphs are indented.

_____ Words are spelled correctly.

SUBSTITUTE TEACHER RESPONSE FORM—NONFICTION WRITING

Group/Class _____

Group/Class _____

Parts of the Writing the Children Did With Ease   **Comments:**

_____ Using the Nonfiction Planner

_____ Writing first drafts

_____ Revising their ideas

_____ Editing their writing

_____ Sharing their writing

Skills for Further Practice   **Comments:**

_____ Using the Nonfiction Planner

_____ Writing first drafts

_____ Revising their ideas

_____ Editing their writing

_____ Sharing their writing

Thank you.

PARENT VOLUNTEER FORM

Name: _____

Child's name: _____

Phone: _____

E-mail address: _____

I prefer to be contacted by _____ phone _____ e-mail

I would be willing to do the following:

_____ Chaperone on field trips

_____ Bake for class events

_____ Buy food or supplies for class events

_____ Work in the classroom with students

_____ Work in the classroom on tasks, such as making bulletin boards, photocopying, checking papers, etc.

_____ Serve as class parent to organize parties and other events

_____ Make materials at home doing tasks such as cutting out things, constructing learning centers, etc.

_____ Maintain the class Web page

_____ Other (please list)

_____

_____

_____

_____

Comments:

_____

VOLUNTEER NOTEBOOK—SUGGESTIONS FOR LISTENING TO A YOUNG CHILD READ

1. If you have not worked with the child before, talk with him or her informally for a few minutes so the child will feel comfortable and safe reading to you.

2. Sit beside the child so that both of you can easily see the book.

_____ If the child has not read the book before, ask the child to look at the front cover and predict what the book is about. When he or she gives an answer, ask, "What made you think that?"

_____ If the child is familiar with the book, ask him or her to tell you what the book is about.

3. As the child reads, use the suggestions in the table on the next page.

4. After the reading is done, ask the child to tell you something about the story: a favorite part, something the story reminded him or her of in real life, or the feelings the story inspired. Notice whether the child understood the story.

5. Make a couple of notes on the Response Sheet.

Error	Appropriate response
If the child makes an error that doesn't affect the meaning ("He went into his HOME," instead of, "He went into his house")	Say nothing at the time of the error. Return to the word after the child has finished the story and help work it out.
If the child comes to a word, stops cold, and can't predict what it is	Ask the child to guess a word that would make sense based on what has been read so far. Help the child check the guess against the letters in the word to see if the guess is correct. If not, try again.
If the child makes an error that affects meaning and becomes confused ("He went to his horse" instead of "He went to his house")	Coach the child to go back to the beginning of the sentence and read it again. If that doesn't help, ask him or her to read to the end of the sentence to see if that helps.
If the child makes an error that affects meaning and keeps on going	Stop and ask if what he or she read makes sense. When the child realizes it doesn't, follow the steps in the previous tip.
If the story is too hard, and the child makes so many errors that it is not making sense	Read the story to the child and ask him or her to chime in with you when he or she can. Reread it and see if the child can read more the second time with your help.

VOLUNTEER NOTEBOOK—RESPONSE
SHEET FOR LISTENING TO CHILDREN READ

Volunteer _____

Name of child who read _____

Story read _____ Date _____

Errors

None or almost none	YES	NO
Most mistakes made sense	YES	NO
Most of the time he or she realized when errors affected meaning and corrected them	YES	NO
Was able to discuss the meaning of the story	YES	NO

Name of child who read _____

Story read _____ Date _____

Errors

None or almost none	YES	NO
Most mistakes made sense	YES	NO
Most of the time he or she realized when errors affected meaning and corrected them	YES	NO
Was able to discuss the meaning of the story	YES	NO

Name of child who read _____

Story read _____ Date _____

Errors

None or almost none	YES	NO
Most mistakes made sense	YES	NO
Most of the time he or she realized when errors affected meaning and corrected them	YES	NO
Was able to discuss the meaning of the story	YES	NO

VOLUNTEER NOTEBOOK—DIRECTIONS FOR READING TO A YOUNG CHILD

- Sit beside the child so he or she can see the pictures and words.

- Look at the cover with the child and read the title. Ask him or her to predict what the book will be about based on the title and cover illustration. Ask why he or she thinks that.

- Begin reading. Read expressively and enthusiastically.

- Stop *only once in awhile* at strategic points to ask the child what he or she thinks will happen next and why.

- When you finish reading, give the child a moment to savor the ending, if that seems like a good idea.

- Initiate a discussion about the book using some of the following questions.

  - What did you think of this story? Why?

  - Did the story remind you of any other book or anything that has ever happened to you?

  - What part did you like best? Why? Do you want to read it again?

  - What parts of the story were hard to understand? Let's talk about them.

Thank you.

VOLUNTEER NOTEBOOK—DIRECTIONS
FOR TALKING WITH A CHILD ABOUT SOMETHING
HE OR SHE HAS WRITTEN

- Sit beside the child so you can both see the writing. Keep the writing in front of the child, however, to signify that the writer owns it. Be sure the child has a pencil to take notes.

- If you have not worked with the child before, talk informally for a few minutes to gain his or her trust and willingness to share.

- Ask what the piece of writing is about. Ask what inspired the child to write about that subject.

- Invite the child to read the piece to you or read the section he or she is working on if it is a long piece.

- Listen attentively without interrupting.

- When the child has finished reading, make some appreciative comments, such as

  - The beginning made me curious about what was going to happen.
  - Your descriptions were so clear, I felt as if I were in your story.
  - Your story reminded me of _____.

- Ask some genuine questions you have about the story. Some examples are:

  - What did Dad say when you told him you had lost your wallet?
  - How did his face look? Could you describe that in your story?
  - Why did the dog suddenly start barking? I didn't understand that part.
  - What are some other choices you could make for how to start your story so people can't wait to read it?

Don't overwhelm the child. Two or three issues to discuss are plenty.

- Ask the child what changes he or she is going to make now. Encourage him or her to jot notes on the paper about the changes. (You should not write on the child's paper.)

- Mention again something you particularly liked about the story and send the child off to revise.

Thank you.

VOLUNTEER SCHEDULING SHEET

Volunteer _____

Date _____

Please work on the following:

Classroom Environment Tasks

_____ Get supplies *(see attached list).*

_____ Redo the bulletin board *(see attached list).*

_____ Bind the attached stories *(see attached list).*

_____ Other _____

_____

Instructional Support Tasks

_____ Listen to the following children read *(see attached directions).*

_____ Read to the following children *(see attached directions).*

_____ Respond to the following children's writing *(see attached directions).*

_____ Other _____

_____

Thank you!

PLANNING FRAME FOR
TRAINING EXPRESSIVE READERS

Warm-Up

- Welcome participants.

- Invite them to share good childhood memories of having parents, siblings, librarians, or others read to them.

What Skills Participants Will Learn

- Selecting a story for reading aloud

- Reviewing and planning the reading of the story

- Using your voice to create interest and enhance comprehension

- Employing effective strategies to keep children's attention

Tips for Reading Expressively

- Outline steps such as the following for participants:

  - Pick a story that you love and think that children will love too.
  - Read through the story initially to yourself to get the meaning.
  - Reread the story to determine how you can use changes in voice, pace, volume, and body language.
  - Find 1 or 2 places where you might want to stop for predictions.
  - Think about how to invite sharing of feelings or other discussion when the story is finished.

Other Tips for Keeping the Attention of Children

- Point out these and any other tips that will help readers:

  - Be sure the length of the story matches the attention span of the audience.
  - Select a story that has engaging pictures.
  - Sit more-restless children near you.
  - Show your excitement.
  - Do not start until everyone is comfortable and settled.
  - In a caring and sensitive way, ask anyone who is restless to move to a less distracting place.

Demonstration of Effective Expressive Reading

• Have volunteers visit a classroom or view a tape that shows how a story can be read effectively.

Discussion of Why the Demonstration Was Effective

• After the demonstration, have the participants verbalize what they saw that relates to the information you shared, as well as other strategies that might have been used.

Selection of a Short Piece to Read Expressively

• Help each participant to select a short story to use with a group of children.

Partner Practice

• Let participants select partners with whom to practice reading their stories.

Opportunity to Read to a Small Group With Peer Feedback

• Set up a chance for participants to practice reading aloud to a small group of children. Let partners observe each other and note effective practices.

Group Discussion of What They Learned During the Practice Opportunity

• Give the group a chance to share their experiences with their practice.

Questions and Answers

• Let participants ask any questions they have at this point.

Note: An alternative to having you and your colleagues deliver this workshop is to see if your media specialist or public librarian might be able to offer the workshop based on his or her training.

PLANNING FRAME FOR TRAINING READING COACHES

Warm-Up

- Give participants a difficult piece of text to read. It could be a passage full of educational jargon or an excerpt from a medical journal, for instance. Ask participants to try to read and comprehend the passage, noticing the techniques they use when they have trouble. After a few minutes of reading time, engage the group in a discussion of how they felt, what they tried to do to help themselves, and how these strategies worked.

What the Participants Will Gain From the Session

- Understanding of what to do to set up a reading session with a child
- Skills they can use with a child who encounters trouble with reading

Observing the Setup for a Reading Session

- Take the participants to a primary-grade class where the teacher or another person who has had training in how to read with a child is introducing a youngster to a new story. Upon returning from the experience, put up an overhead that describes story introduction steps and ask participants how they saw these elements used.
  - Putting the child at ease with informal conversation
  - Sitting so that both the child and the coach can easily see the book
  - Asking the child to look at the cover and title and do a picture walk to make predictions about the content of the book

Present Tips on What to Do When a Child Makes an Error

- Explain that errors help coaches see what a child already knows and what he or she is ready to learn next. Hand out the chart on the next page and go over actions to take for each kind of error.

- Give teachers a chance to observe and discuss a live demonstration or tape of a coach and child working through errors.

Practicing the Techniques

- Because this is a role that requires more expertise than some others, it is important to provide several practice and feedback session for coaches.

Error	Appropriate response
If the child makes an error that doesn't affect the meaning ("He went into his HOME," instead of, "He went into his house")	Say nothing at the time of the error. Return to the word after the child has finished the story and help work it out.
If the child comes to a word, stops cold, and can't predict what it is	Ask the child to guess a word that would make sense based on what has been read so far. Help the child check the guess against the letters in the word to see if the guess is correct. If not, try again.
If the child makes an error that affects meaning and becomes confused ("He went to his horse" instead of "He went to his house")	Coach the child to go back to the beginning of the sentence and read it again. If that doesn't help, ask him or her to read to the end of the sentence to see if that helps.
If the child makes an error that affects meaning and keeps on going	Stop and ask if what he or she read makes sense. When the child realizes it doesn't, follow the steps in the previous tip.
If the story is too hard, and the child makes so many errors that it is not making sense	Read the story to the child and ask him or her to chime in with you when he or she can. Reread it and see if the child can read more the second time with your help.

PLANNING FRAME FOR
TRAINING WRITING COACHES

Warm-Up

- Welcome participants.
- Encourage volunteers to imagine that you asked them to share a piece of writing with the group for their critique. Have them identify specific fears they might have about doing this.

Explanation of Which Skills Will Be Addressed

- Differentiating between writing and editing skills
- Identifying several positive comments to make to each author
- Planning 2 or 3 focus points to discuss with an author
- Determining how to discuss these focus points with the author
- Honoring the author's right to make final decisions

Observation of Teacher Coaching Young Writer

- Arrange to have volunteer coaches watch live or videotaped teacher coaching sessions with 1 or more young authors.

Listing by Participants of Effective Techniques They Observed

- Engage the volunteers in a discussion of effective techniques they observed. List these on a chart.

Discussion by Presenter of Additional Tips

- Point out any additional tips that the observers did not notice or that were not employed during this session. These may include the following:

  - Find several points on which you can genuinely compliment the writer.
  - Focus on just a couple of coaching points rather than overwhelming the child.
  - Ask questions to inspire the child to think about his or her piece rather than telling the child how to change the writing.
  - Avoid taking the paper out of the child's possession. Let the author hold onto the paper and make any changes or notes on it.
  - Let the child make the final decision about which changes to implement.

Opportunity to Plan a Coaching Session for a Child

- Distribute a piece of children's writing to each participant. Ask volunteers to work in pairs to find several compliments to make on each paper. Have each identify one teaching point and plan how to discuss that point with the author.

Implementing the Coaching Plan

- Provide an opportunity for the pairs of coaches to meet with the authors of their papers and implement their plans.

Peer and Presenter Input

- Provide positive reinforcement and additional ideas to try for each coach.

Addition of Other Techniques to the List

- See if the volunteers have other points to add to their list of techniques based on their practice experience.

Questions and Answers

- Encourage participants to ask questions to clarify and extend their understanding of the coaching process.

Note: It is a good idea to reproduce the list of tips that the group generated so that each coach may have a copy for reference.

PLANNING FRAME FOR TRAINING EDITORS

Warm-Up

- Welcome participants.
- Give each volunteer a card with a comment such as:
  - Grammar and spelling are the most important part of learning to write.
  - Grammar and spelling are not that important as long as you can understand the meaning of what was written.
  - Children should be given lots of time to write in their own way before formal spelling and grammar are imposed on them.
  - Youngsters should learn the correct way to write from the beginning or they will acquire bad habits.
- Give the volunteers 3 to 5 minutes to talk with a partner about their reactions to their cards.
- Debrief the activity by talking about the district's or school's philosophy regarding instruction on laguage mechanics. Beware! This can be an emotional issue for many people, so be ready to explain the philosophy with clarity and conviction. Also, save yourself and your volunteers distress by choosing editors who are in tune with your program.

Discussion of Skills That Participants Will Acquire

- Ability to decide how to review papers for language mechanics
- Knowledge of the way to mark areas for improvement
- Ability to communicate with youngsters about editing

Modeling of How to Mark Papers

- Put up an overhead transparency of a child's writing that includes some language mechanics and spelling errors.
- Talk through how you would choose 3 types of errors on which to focus so as not to overwhelm or discourage the child.
- Demonstrate how you would mark these areas for growth in a positive, constructive way.

Demonstration of Editing Conference

- Have a teacher conduct an editing conference with a child.

Discussion of Skills Observed

- Engage participants in a conversation about how the teacher focused on a manageable number of editing skills.
- Ask participants to identify techniques the teacher used to preserve the child's dignity and maintain his or her interest and confidence in writing.

Practice

- Give pairs of participants papers to mark and prepare for conferences.
- Have participants either conduct editing conferences with the authors of their papers or role-play conferences with each other.

Input From Observers

- Encourage partners to compliment each other on successes and make suggestions for ideas to try in the future.

Closure

- Engage participants in creating a "do's and don'ts" list for Editors. Copy and distribute the list to all "graduates" of the workshop.

PLANNING FRAME FOR TRAINING DISCUSSION FACILITATORS

Warm-Up

- Engage participants in discussing a recent movie that most have seen. As they talk, unobtrusively jot down the kinds of information they are discussing. After the conversation dies down, point out that none of them engaged in a "school" discussion involving anyone asking questions such as, "Who was the main character?"

What Participants Will Learn

- How to start a book discussion
- When to step in and when to step back and let youngsters lead
- Technique for debriefing a book discussion

    (Volunteers will be successful only if you have the children well trained in book discussion before they work with the coach.)

Present Tips for Facilitating a Book Discussion

- Start with an open-ended question such as: "What did you think of this story?" or "Did the story remind you of any other book or anything that has ever happened to you or anyone you know?"
- Let children lead with the points they have prepared to bring up in discussion.
- Jump into the conversation only when discussion has dried up and you have waited 10 seconds to see if anyone else restarts it. If it is necessary for you to say something, use another open-ended question or comment such as, "What did you find confusing or hard to understand?"
- While discussion is under way, jot down notes about how each child contributed.

Demonstration

- Invite participants to sit as silent observers of a book discussion. Have them take notes what they see and jot down questions.

Discussion of Demonstration

- After the demonstration, give participants plenty of time to comment on their observations and ask questions.

Practice

- Give each participant a short piece of literature to read.
- Have participants work in pairs to decide how they might start the discussion and what kinds of restart questions or comments they might have ready, if needed.

Share and Provide Peer and Presenter Feedback

- Allocate some time to sharing the results of the partner work.

DIRECTIONS FOR BOOK BINDING

Materials

Cardboard (from gift, cereal, or other boxes)
Plastic tape
Self-adhesive paper or cloth
Clear tape

Instructions

1. Cut 2 pieces of cardboard slightly larger than the paper on which the story is written.

2. Cut 2 pieces of self-adhesive cloth or paper, each of which is slightly larger than the cardboard. Cover the cardboard pieces with these. Fold in the excess neatly on the back side of the cover.

3. Cut a piece of plastic tape and put the 2 pieces of covered cardboard together.

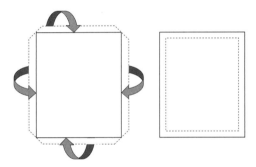

4. Cut another piece of plastic tape and put it over the 1 in Step 3.

5. Use clear tape to fix in each page of the story.

Other notes to the bookbinder:

BULLETIN BOARD ARTIST'S PLANNING SHEET

Rough sketch of art and lettering:

Exact wording to appear:

Location of supplies:

CORWIN
PRESS

The Corwin Press logo—a raven striding across an open book—represents the happy union of courage and learning. We are a professional-level publisher of books and journals for K-12 educators, and we are committed to creating and providing resources that embody these qualities. Corwin's motto is "Success for All Learners."